Original Goodness

Also by Eknath Easwaran

★

Gandhi the Man
The Bhagavad Gita for Daily Living
Meditation
Mantram Handbook
Dialogue with Death
The Supreme Ambition
God Makes the Rivers to Flow
A Man to Match His Mountains
Love Never Faileth
Thousand Names of Vishnu
Conquest of Mind

★

Classics of Indian Spirituality Series:
The Bhagavad Gita
The Dhammapada
The Upanishads

ORIGINAL GOODNESS

EKNATH EASWARAN

Nilgiri Press

© 1989 by the Blue Mountain Center of Meditation
All rights reserved. Printed in the United States of America
ISBN: cloth, 0–915132–57–5; paper, 0–915132–56–7
First printing June 1989
The Blue Mountain Center of Meditation, founded in Berkeley in 1960
by Eknath Easwaran, publishes books on how to lead the spiritual life in
the home and the community. For information please write to
Nilgiri Press, Box 477, Petaluma, California 94953

⊗ The paper used in this publication meets the minimum requirements
of American National Standard for Information Services – Permanence
of Paper for Printed Library Materials, ANSI Z39.48-1984.

Library of Congress Cataloging-in-Publication Data:

Easwaran, Eknath.
    Original goodness / by Eknath Easwaran.
    1. Spiritual Life. 2. Meditation.   3. Beatitudes.
    I. Title.
  BL624.E175 1989 291.4'48 89–15931
    ISBN 0–915132–56–7 (alk. paper)
    ISBN 0–915132–57–5 (hard : alk. paper)

Table of Contents

Original Goodness

*I have spoken at times of a light in the soul, a
light that is uncreated and uncreatable . . . to the
extent that we can deny ourselves and turn away
from created things, we shall find our unity and
blessing in that little spark in the soul, which
neither space nor time touches.*
– Meister Eckhart

THESE WORDS, ADDRESSED TO ordinary people
in a quiet German-speaking town almost seven hundred
years ago, testify to a discovery about the nature of the
human spirit as revolutionary as Einstein's theories about
the nature of the universe. If truly understood, that discovery would transform the world we live in at least as
radically as Einstein's theories changed the world of
science. "We have grasped the mystery of the atom,"
General Omar Bradley once said, "and rejected the Sermon on the Mount. . . . Ours is a world of nuclear giants
and ethical infants." If we could grasp the mystery of
Eckhart's "uncreated light in the soul" – surely no more
abstruse than relativity! – the transformation in our
thinking would set our world right side up.

Meister or "Master" Eckhart – the title attests to his scholarship, but seems to fit even better his spiritual authority – lived almost exactly at the same time and for the same span as Dante, and both seem born to those lofty regions of the spirit that do not belong to any particular culture, religion, or age but are universal. Yet, also like Dante, Eckhart expressed perfectly something essential about his times. The end of the thirteenth century was a period of intense turmoil in Europe, and the Rhine valley, where Eckhart was born, was the breeding ground of various popular religious societies which alarmed conventional Christians. Yet a God who could be known personally and a path by which to reach him were what an increasing number of people yearned for, and Eckhart's passionate sermons, straining to convey the Absolute in the words of the street and marketplace, became immensely popular.

And what did he teach? Essentially, four principles that Spinoza would later call the Perennial Philosophy, because they have been taught from age to age in culture after culture:

★ First, there is a "light in the soul that is uncreated and uncreatable": unconditioned, universal, deathless; in religious language, a divine core of personality which cannot be separated from God. Eckhart is precise: this is not what the English language calls the "soul," but some essence in the soul that lies at the very center of consciousness. As Saint Catherine of Genoa put it, "My *me* is God: nor do I know my selfhood except in God." In Indian mysticism this divine core is called simply *atman*, "the Self."

★ Second, this divine essence can be *realized*. It is not an abstraction, and it need not – Eckhart would say *must* not – remain hidden under the covering of our everyday personality. It can and should be *dis*covered, so that its presence becomes a reality in daily life.

★ Third, this discovery is life's real and highest goal. Our supreme purpose in life is not to make a fortune, nor to pursue pleasure, nor to write our name on history, but to discover this spark of the divine that is in our hearts.

★ Last, when we realize this goal, we discover simultaneously that the divinity within ourselves is one and the same in all – all individuals, all creatures, all of life.

Words can certainly be ambiguous with ideas such as these, and "mysticism" is no exception. In this book, a mystic is one who not only espouses these principles of the Perennial Philosophy but *lives* them, whose every action reflects the wisdom and selfless love that are the hallmark of one who has made this supreme discovery. Such a person has made the divine a reality in every moment of life, and that reality shines through whatever he or she may do or say – and that is the real test. It is not occult fancies or visions or esoteric discourses that mark the mystic, but an unbroken awareness of the presence of God in all creatures. The signs are clear: unfailing compassion, fearlessness, equanimity, and the unshakable knowledge, based on direct, personal experience, that all the treasures and pleasures of this world together are worth nothing if one has not found the uncreated light at the center of the soul.

These are demanding criteria, and few people in the history of the world can be said to have met them. I shall often refer to these men and women collectively as "the great mystics," not to obscure their differences, but to emphasize this tremendous undercurrent of the spirit that keeps resurfacing from age to age to remind us of our real legacy as human beings.

On this legacy the mystics are unanimous. We are made, the scriptures of all religions assure us, in the image of God. Nothing can change that original goodness. Whatever mistakes we have made in the past, whatever problems we may have in the present, in every one of us this "uncreated spark in the soul" remains untouched, ever pure, ever perfect. Even if we try with all our might to douse or hide it, it is always ready to set our personality ablaze with light.

When I was growing up in South India, just half an hour's walk from my home was a lotus pond so thickly overlaid with glossy leaves and gleaming rose and white blossoms that you could scarcely see the water. One of the Sanskrit names for this most exquisite of flowers is *pankaja,* "born from the mud." In the murky depths of the pond a seed takes root. Then a long, wavering strand reaches upward, groping through the water toward the glimmer of light above. From the water a bud emerges. Warmed by the sun's rays, it slowly opens out and forms a perfect chalice to catch and hold the dazzling light of the sun.

The lotus makes a beautiful symbol for the core of goodness in every human being. Though we are born of human clay, it reminds us, each of us has the latent capacity to reach and grow toward heaven until we shine with the reflected glory of our Maker.

Early in the first century, a Greek Father of the Church, Origen, referred to this core of goodness as both a spark and a divine seed – a seed that is sown deep in consciousness by the very fact of our being human, made in the image of our Creator. "Even though it is covered up," Origen explains,

> because it is God that has sowed this seed in us, pressed it in, begotten it, it cannot be extirpated or die out; it glows and sparkles, burning and giving light, and always it moves upward toward God.

Eckhart seized the metaphor and dared take it to the full limits it implies:

> The seed of God is in us. Given an intelligent and hard-working farmer, it will thrive and grow up to God,

whose seed it is, and accordingly its fruits will be God-nature. Pear seeds grow into pear trees, nut seeds into nut trees, and God-seed into God.

"Its fruit will be God-nature"! What promise could be more revolutionary? Yet Eckhart, like other great mystics of the Church before and after him, does no more than assure us of his personal experience. The seed *is* there, and the ground is fertile. Nothing is required but diligent gardening to bring into existence the God-tree: a life that proclaims the original goodness in all creation.

The implications of this statement are far-reaching. Rightly understood, they can lift the most oppressive burden of guilt, restore any loss of self-esteem. For if goodness is our real core, goodness that can be hidden but never taken away, then goodness is not something we have to *get*. We do not have to figure out how to make ourselves good; all we need do is remove what covers the goodness that is already there.

To be sure, removing these coverings is far from easy. Original goodness does not mean that you are already divine and just do not know it – much less that, as some New Age writers put it, "you yourself are God." Having a core of goodness does not prevent the rest of personality from being a monumental nuisance. But the very concept of original goodness can transform our lives. It does not deny what traditional religion calls sin; it simply reminds us that before original sin was original innocence. *That* is our real nature. Everything else – all our habits, our conditioning, our past mistakes – is a mask. A mask can hide a face completely; like that frightful iron contraption in Dumas's novel, it can be excruciating to wear and nearly impossible to remove. But the very nature of a mask is that it *can* be removed. This is the promise and the purpose of all spiritual disciplines: to take off the mask that hides our real face.

★

It is said that the English astronomer Sir Arthur Eddington, when he announced to a bewildered world the first experiments vindicating Einstein's theories, was asked by journalists, "Is it true that only three people in the world understand the theory of relativity?" Eddington took his time, then replied in carefully puzzled tones, "Who is the third?"

That is roughly where we stand today with this discovery of original goodness. I began by saying that if Eckhart's words were truly understood, they could turn our world right side up. Yet the same has rightly been said of the Sermon on the Mount, which has never been in danger of enjoying sweeping acceptance. Mystics speak boldly and call us all to follow; but the price is high, and few want to listen.

But from time to time mysticism does flourish, often in response to some deep need in a troubled age. The late Middle Ages must have been such a period in Western Christendom, for it fostered one of the most remarkable flowerings of the Perennial Philosophy the world has known. The amazing popularity of Eckhart's sermons, delivered with the ardor and humanity of a Saint Francis but about as accessible to the average person as a talk on quantum mechanics, is just one piece of the evidence. From roughly 1200 to 1400, from Saint Francis himself to Thomas a Kempis, there arose not only some two dozen of Christianity's greatest mystics but also a wave of popular response among the common people.

What has this to do with us at the end of the twentieth century? A great deal, I think. The fourteenth century was a time of turbulence not unlike that of our own age – "a distant mirror," to use the historian Barbara Tuchman's phrase. The popular appeal of a man like Eckhart, a quiet friar who did no more to rouse a following than preach in church about things the intellect can scarcely grasp, is evidence that however abstract the concept of original goodness may seem, ordinary people do need and respond to the idea of a spark of the divine in their own soul. The reason is simple: nothing else can fill the hunger in the human heart. Even today, with abundance within reach for more people than ever, we need something more than the physical world can offer.

Last Christmastime I sat in a café inside a fashionable department store, watching the shoppers come and go. Most of them, I thought, had not come to buy things they already wanted. It was as if they had come looking for something to want – something that might fill a nameless need, even if only for a moment. Above the glittering displays a poster bearing the name of the mall promised proudly, "The Fantasy Is Real."

To me, it is a comment on the nobility of human nature that even in the midst of such a smorgasbord of things and activities and sensations, we still feel a need for something real. For although modern civilization has made remarkable progress in many fields, it has neglected others that are vital for well-being. "Progress is a good thing," said Ogden Nash, "but it has been going on too long." Material progress does improve well-being up to a point; but beyond that point, instead of lifting us upward, it only leads us around in circles. Making things, buying and selling them, piling them up, repairing them, trying to figure out how to get rid of them permanently: for sensitive people, boredom with this carnival cycle began some time ago. A consumer culture is not the goal of life.

None of us need feel guilty if we have been caught in the games of profit and pleasure that industrial civilization holds up for us as life's goal. These are stages that a society goes through, just as a child plays and then discards what he or she outgrows. What matters is not that we may have made mistakes in the pursuit of physical satisfactions;

what is important is to learn from these mistakes as quickly as we can that wealth, possessions, power, and pleasure have never brought lasting satisfaction to any human being. Our needs go too deep to be satisfied by anything that comes and goes. Nothing but spiritual fulfillment can fill the void in our hearts.

Today, I think, millions of people find themselves at a crossroads, forced to ask penetrating questions that in simpler times were the province only of philosophers: *What is life for? Why am I here? Is there more to me than this body? Is happiness a foolish dream; can it actually be found without closing my eyes to what I see?* New Age philosophies, and new sciences too, search for answers. But do we really need new answers to enter a new age? The questions are frankly old, and human nature has not changed. Are the answers of religion out of date? Have we forgotten the daring pioneers of the spirit who discovered and tapped a reservoir of joy, wisdom, and healing within – and who insist that we can tap it too?

We *have* forgotten, is the delicate answer, and it is not entirely our fault. The reason why we do not learn of these discoveries is that they are so rarely understood – cannot be understood, in fact, except by those who try to live them; and if understanding Einstein was difficult when relativity was new, shall we expect to learn in school about things "uncreated and uncreatable"? Among the disturbing trends of our age is the tendency to identify the human being as nothing more than a biochemical entity and then argue, "There is no such thing as spirit. How can the center of personality be something that 'time and space cannot touch'?"

Yet even this skepticism is not new; in a sense, it is nothing more than the modern echo of an age-old doubt. As Hans Denk, a German mystic of the sixteenth century, exclaimed to God, "Men flee from thee and say they cannot find thee. They turn their backs and say they cannot see thee. They stop their ears and say they cannot hear thee."

Centuries before, Eckhart had urged:

You need not seek God here or there: he is no farther off than the door of the heart. There he stands and waits and waits until he finds you ready to open and let him in. You need not call him from a distance; to wait until you open for him is harder for him than for you. He needs you a thousand times more than you can need him. *Your opening and his entering are but one moment.*

One of my deepest desires is to convey this simple truth to the millions of people today who seem at a loss for what to live for, and especially to the young. The president of the American Association of Suicidology estimated in 1986 that half a million of our teenagers attempt suicide each year. In a free and affluent society such as ours, why would so many of our children come to the conclusion that their lives are not worth pursuing? It is tempting to point a finger at specific causes like drugs, but the president of the Youth Suicide National Center in Washington looks deeper. Our young people are profoundly troubled, she says, because "their sense of future is gone."

Global threats like environmental disaster and nuclear war are enough to undermine anyone's sense of future. Yet even more damaging, in my opinion, is the lack of a sustaining purpose. With a higher goal, human beings can face any challenge. But without a goal, the spirit withers, and when the natural idealism of the young is blocked, their energy eventually breaks through into uncontrolled and often self-destructive channels. Most young people I know do not really want an easy life. They long for *challenge:* real challenges, all the bigger because their capacities are so huge. All they ask is something to live for. But we have become a culture without large goals, with nothing but material abundance to offer the hunger in their hearts.

In almost every country and every age, there are a few men and women who see through the game of personal satisfaction and ask themselves, "Is this all? I want something much bigger to live for, something much loftier to desire." Nothing transient can appease this hunger. It touches something very deep in us, caught as we are in our predicament as human beings: partly physical, partly spiritual, trying to feel at home in the world into which we have been born. What is the reason for this gnawing dissatisfaction? The world's great spiritual traditions all give the same answer: we are not wholly at home in this world of change and death. The body may belong, but the spirit is in exile here, a wanderer, a stranger in a strange land. And we long for home.

In Western symbols it is Eden that stands for "the soul's true home" from which we have somehow been banished. In this sense, Eden is not so much a place as a state of consciousness. We may conceive of the Creation in time and space, but it is essentially our separation from our native state of original goodness which marks our advent into the world as seemingly separate individuals – in traditional language, the Fall.

Yet although we feel exiled from this state, our exile is only apparent. Like the rabbi in the Hasidic tale who walks back and forth over buried treasure every day without ever guessing what is beneath his feet, every moment we pass unaware over the core of goodness in our hearts.

The scientific account of the creation of the universe suggests a modern metaphor for Eden and the Fall. Before the Big Bang, physicists tell us, all the matter in the universe must have been compressed in an incomprehensible point, before time and outside space. Matter and energy were one in that primal state. Even in the first few seconds of creation, the universe was mostly light. Ordinary matter, in the infinite variety we experience today, devolved from pure energy flung into space and time by the explosion of creation.

In the same way we might speak of Eden as a state of pure, unitary consciousness, logically prior to the differentiation between matter and mind. Just as there was a point before time when all matter and energy in the universe was one, there is a state of awareness in which all creation is one. The Fall is then the Big Bang: the process of individuation, which seems to scatter this unitary consciousness into fragments, leaving each of us with a shard of Eden in our hearts.

Physicists tell us that the elements created in the Big Bang are present throughout the universe, from the soil in our gardens to the gas clouds of the farthest galaxy. Many years ago, when people were lining up in San Francisco to see a rock our astronauts had brought from the moon, I picked up a rock from the road and thought to myself, "This too is a moon rock. There's no difference." Fragments from the Big Bang lie all around us, just as in distant stars. In the same way, the mystics say, a trace of our original divinity is present in every creature. In some, like Saint Francis of Assisi, it is highly revealed, in others it is more heavily veiled; but that divinity is present throughout creation.

Jewish mysticism puts this idea into haunting imagery. Shekinah, the Presence of God, is dispersed throughout creation in every creature, like sparks scattered from the pure flame of spirit that is the Lord. And each spark, seemingly alone in the darkness of blind matter, wanders this world in exile, seeking to return to its divine source.

Yet the Fall is not just an event that took place in 4004 B.C. It is still going on. Just as radio telescopes can pick up faint echoes of the Big Bang, we hear echoes of our fall into separateness every day. Superjets may have brought

New York and Paris closer than ever, but I doubt that individuals have ever been more distant. And like island universes, we seem to be rushing apart at an accelerating speed. We are increasingly alienated from others and from ourselves.

In this interpretation, when Adam and Eve ate the fruit of the tree of knowledge, what they tasted is what the Sanskrit language calls *ahamkara:* literally, "I-maker," the sense of being "an island unto oneself" – something separate from the rest of life, with unique needs and peremptory claims.

This is a highly tempting fruit. If I were a playwright, I could write an entertaining play in which the serpent comes and sells the apple of separateness to Adam and Eve. "Hey, try this! Nothing could be more natural: just be yourself and take care of number one. You can have your food just the way you like it. You can decorate your apartment any old way you choose. You can play only the music you like, at any hour of the day or night. You can wear any kind of clothes you like. You can make any amount of money, by any means, and spend it on anything under the sun. Avoid people you don't like; you can even keep them off your block. Go to sleep when you want, get up when you want . . . you don't have to care for anybody!" That is the serpent's message, and among other things it makes us ideal, insatiable consumers. My sympathies are all with Adam and Eve when they fell for this. Don't we twentieth-century men and women, sophisticated as they come, go on falling all too easily for the same old apple?

To me, the serpent is not a villainous figure. He is simply an effective salesman. The serpent was only doing his job; he *had* to sell. "Don't blame me," he might well protest. "They didn't have to buy. I was able to tempt them because they were temptable." Talk about smooth! The word *serpent* comes from a Sanskrit word which means to slither about, to be smooth in one's movements: so smooth that nobody suspected there was a price to pay for what he offered, and exorbitant finance charges too.

For what seems such tempting fruit at the beginning slowly begins to cause stomachache. Separateness becomes a habit and finally a compulsive state of mind. This is a tragic development, for a person who can think only of himself, someone who explodes when things do not go her way, is a fragile, alienated, and very lonely individual. And the tragedy does not stop there; that is why I said that the Fall is still continuing. In the end, it is this driving sense of separateness – *I, I, I; my* needs, *my* wants, apart from all the rest of life – that is responsible for all the wars in history, all the violence, all the exploitation of other human beings, and even the exploitation of the planet that threatens our future today.

Yet what we seek when we fall for the serpent's pitch is very natural. What *do* we want from life, judging not by our words but by our actions? Very simple, basic things, common to all. We want to love and to be loved. We want happiness and fulfillment, though we may have differing ideas of what that means. We want a place in life, a way of belonging, a sense of purpose, the achievement of worthy goals – whatever it takes; otherwise life is an empty show. And, of course, we want never to die.

These are natural desires, and no amount of experience can erase them from our hearts. Why? Because these are the demands of Eckhart's "little spark" of the spirit, and that spark is real and inalienable: "nearer to us than our very body," as the Sufis say, "dearer than our very life."

These yearnings are not wrong, then. What happens is that we interpret them wrongly. They are messages from the spirit which have somehow got scrambled by the world of matter, and we lack the decoder by which to understand. That scrambling is what Hindu mysticism means by the much-misunderstood word *maya:* the wishful, willful illusion that the thirst in our hearts is physical and can somehow be slaked by physical experience. We wander searching for the right things in the wrong places, seeking Eden in the world of the senses, and life itself seems to delight in frustrating us.

"The soul is a pilgrim," said John Ruysbroeck, one of the great Rhineland mystics who succeeded Eckhart, "for it sees its country." But until we glimpse our "soul's true home," we are not so much pilgrims as tourists. Being a traveler is one thing, but no one really likes to be a tourist. Nothing is ever quite right: the food, the beds, the chairs, the customs. We shake our heads and mutter under our breath the universal tourist's complaint: "Back home . . ."

Deep below the level of conscious awareness, the world's mystical traditions tell us, that refrain goes on constantly in every heart. *Back home . . .* And a brilliant contemporary of Eckhart's, Mechthild of Magdeburg, gives us the reason. "The soul is made of love," she exclaims – made of love, just as the body is made of flesh – "and must ever strive to return to love. Therefore, it can never find rest nor happiness in other things. It must lose itself in love. By its very nature it must seek God, who is love."

In everyone there is this inward tug, this call to return. But because we are turned outward, our hearing gets confused. The call seems to be coming from outside. What we seek is always just around the corner . . . and when we reach the corner, it has ducked out of sight down the block. Yet human nature is so strong that even after turning corners a thousand times, we still say, "The thousand and first – that's going to be the one!" Life becomes a pilgrimage around corners.

But there comes a time when corners no longer beckon. We know from bitter experience that they only hide blind alleys. This juncture is critical; for once one reaches it, nothing on earth can satisfy for long. Those with drive may plunge into restless activity. The more frustrated they feel, the more things they try – globe-trotting, solo climbing, cars, clothes, casinos, commodities futures. But the desire to wrest meaning from life only grows more urgent as frustration mounts.

Later, looking back, this utter restlessness may prove to be the first touch of what traditional religion calls grace. It means that a person has grown too big to be satisfied with petty satisfactions that come and go. But the crisis is real. If we do not understand the message, frustration can turn desperate or self-destructive – not only for an individual, but for a whole society. Each age has its own kind of suffering, the natural consequences of mistaken values it pursues, and the suffering of our industrial age is loneliness, alienation, and despair. Alienation can cause terrible harm; for it is when we feel isolated and alone that we lose sensitivity to others, and obsession with private desires and fears fills up our world. Walk the streets of any inner city today and you will see the fruits of separateness all around you, the anguish of a society in which even children and the aged are cut adrift and left on their own.

There comes a time in the growth of civilizations, as with individuals, when the life-and-death questions of material existence have been answered, yet the soul still thirsts and physical challenges cease to satisfy. Then we stand at a crossroads: for without meaningful aspiration, the human being turns destructive. Spiritual fulfillment is an evolutionary imperative. Like a snake that must shed its skin to grow, our industrial civilization must shed its material outlook or strangle in outgrown ideals whose constructive potential has been spent.

In the end, then, life itself turns us inward – "away from created things," as Eckhart says, to "find our unity and blessing in that little spark in the soul." The end of the Fall is the Return. Alienation is the heartache of feeling out of place in a senseless universe. Its purpose is to turn us homeward, and all experience ultimately conspires to that end. "Whether you like it or not, whether you know it or not," Eckhart assures us, "secretly Nature seeks and hunts and tries to ferret out the track in which God may be found."

This is a most compassionate view of human nature. Even when we are busy accumulating possessions with which to feather our little nest, planning a hilltop castle with garage space for half a dozen new cars, Eckhart would say we are really looking for God. We think, "If I can fix up my place just right, with a little bar and sauna in my room and my own entertainment center at my fingertips, *then* I'll feel at home!" But we will never be at home except in Eden.

"The man of God never rejoices," Eckhart declares. We think, "Just what I suspected! Every saint is really a sourpuss." But then he explains himself: "The man of God never rejoices, because he is joy itself."

When all hostility, all resentment, all greed and fear and insecurity are erased from your mind, the state that remains is pure joy. When we become established in that state, we live in joy always.

That state of joy, hidden at the very center of consciousness, is the Eden to which the long journey of spiritual seeking leads. There, the mystics of all religions agree, we uncover our original goodness. We don't have to buy it; we don't have to create it; we don't have to pour it in; we don't even have to be worthy of it. This native goodness is the essential core of human nature.

The purpose of all valid spiritual disciplines, whatever the religion from which they spring, is to enable us to return to this native state of being – not after death but here and now, in unbroken awareness of the divinity within us and throughout creation. Theologians may quarrel, but the mystics of the world speak the same language, and the practices they follow lead to the same goal.

It is in this light that this book presents the Beatitudes – the series of eight verses from the Sermon on the Mount which begins, in Matthew's version, "Blessed are the poor in spirit, for theirs is the kingdom of heaven." Each chapter takes one of the Beatitudes as a spiritual law which has the power to uncover the "uncreated light" in the depths of personality when we allow it to shape our thoughts and actions.

I want to make it clear, however, that this is not an attempt at Biblical commentary. I am content to leave explication and exegesis to scholars. In these chapters I simply comment on some of what the Beatitudes mean to me after decades of effort in trying to translate them into my life. I have chosen Matthew over Luke not for any theological reason, but because these are the words written on my memory half a century ago by a man I revered: the principal of a small Catholic college in Kerala, South India, who taught me through his personal example what Christ's teachings mean in daily living.

Meditation

Whatever our religious beliefs – or even if formalized religion is anathema – it is possible for every one of us to uncover the core of goodness of which Eckhart speaks. It has nothing to do with theology and everything to do with practice. In other words, what we say we believe in is not so important; what matters is what we actually do – and, even more, what we actually are. "As we think in our hearts, so we are." Goodness *is* in us; our job is simply to get deep into our consciousness and begin removing what stands in the way.

Doing this, however, is no small task. I would go to the extent of saying that there is no way to accomplish this today except through the systematic practice of meditation.

How can I make such a sweeping statement? Because I mean something very particular and practical by the word "meditation." Although it is a spiritual discipline, meditation stands above the differences that define the world's great religions. Meditation is not dogma or doctrine or metaphysics; it is a powerful tool. Everyone can use a shovel, regardless of his views on the dignity of hand labor. Similarly, everyone can use meditation to dig into consciousness and change it to conform with her highest ideals.

On the one hand, then, when I talk about meditation, I am referring to a specific interior discipline which is found in every major religion, though called by different names. (Catholic writers, for example, use terms like "contemplation" or "interior prayer," reserving the word "meditation" for another very specific spiritual practice.) So when I say that meditation is necessary for uncovering the God-seed in your heart, you can see that I am not closing a door on anyone at all.

On the other hand, a great many activities called meditation are quite different from what I mean, so it is important to be clear.

When I first came to this country from India on the Fulbright exchange in 1959, practically no one talked about meditation. I could use the word without much concern that my audience might misunderstand. Today the scene is very different. If you want to learn about meditation, you can go to a library and find more than a hundred books in print on the subject, not counting the articles in popular magazines. And if you look in the Yellow Pages, you can find institutions from karate schools to hospitals offering to teach you how to meditate – each in a different way. With so much activity on the stage, I have found it necessary to say precisely what I mean or court confusion.

First, meditation as I teach and practice it is not a relaxation technique. I respect teachers and health professionals who use the word in this way, but we have the testimony of great mystics from every culture and every age that meditation requires strenuous effort. If you expect to find it easy going, you are going to be disappointed.

True, meditation does relieve the tensions of the day. But so does a ten-mile run, which is a lot of work at the time. And meditation does go on relieving tension at a deeper and deeper level, as knots and conflicts in personality are undone. But in general, especially at the beginning, meditation is work; the rewards come during the rest of the day.

Second, although there are highly respectable schools of meditation which rightly emphasize that their goal is not relaxation but awareness, their methods often involve heightening awareness of some physiological activity like breathing. I respect these methods in the hands of an experienced teacher, but to me meditation is essentially an interior discipline. The mind needs to turn inward, and to do this we have to forget the body during the period of meditation. (Interestingly enough, it is just when we forget about the body that it functions at its best.)

Third, meditation as I teach it is not visualization, nor is it drifting in a reverie and imagining pleasant things. It is not letting the mind wander, "guided" or unguided, nor observing thoughts flow by in quiet detachment. If we could really watch our thoughts in that manner, our emotions would have no power to seize hold of us – which means we would never lose our temper, never think a hostile thought, never feel afraid.

Finally, it is important to distinguish meditation from disciplined reflection on a particular theme. I stress this because many eminent spiritual figures have used the word in this way. Reflection on a spiritual topic can yield valuable insights; but for the vast majority of us, reflection is an activity on the surface level of the mind. To transform personality we need to go much, much deeper. We need a way to get eventually into the unconscious itself, where our contrary thoughts and deepest desires arise, and make changes *there*. That is the purpose of meditation.

So what *is* meditation? It is the regular, systematic training of attention to turn inward and dwell continuously on a single focus within consciousness, until, after many years, we become so absorbed in the object of our contemplation that while we are meditating, we forget ourselves completely. In that moment, when we may be said to be empty of ourselves, we are utterly full of what we are dwelling on. This is the central principle of meditation: we become what we meditate on.

Meditation, then, means training the mind: teaching our thoughts to go where we tell them and to obey themselves while they are there, much as we train a puppy. We begin by learning how to train our attention – both in meditation and during the rest of the day – until eventually we make our mind calm, clear, and concentrated as a laser, which we can direct and focus at will. This is a tremendous skill, as you can appreciate if you have ever tried to take your mind off some nagging personal problem and concentrate completely on the job at hand. In any particular subject, this capacity for one-pointed attention is the essence of genius; anyone who has it is bound to make a mark in his or her field. But when you have this kind of mastery over your attention in everything you do, you have a genius for life itself: unshakable security, clear judgment, deep personal relationships, compassion that no adversity can break down.

Yet this is only the beginning of where meditation can

lead. In its deeper stages, meditation means reconditioning the unconscious itself: taming the most powerful forces we can encounter, our own desires. Below the surface of personality, all of us are torn by conflicting urges; that is the human condition. In training the mind to dwell on a lofty ideal, we gradually drive that ideal deep into consciousness and release the will to translate it into action. Conflicts in personality are resolved, so that what we believe in, what we do, and what we think become one. Training attention brings mastery of most personal problems, but this reconditioning of the unconscious brings a complete transformation of personality.

When I say these things before a new audience, I always expect some intellectual questions and objections. But every now and then, someone will come to me afterward and say, "Great! But what do I actually *do?*" I want to throw my arms around such people and exclaim, "Oh, thank you for asking!" That is just the kind of question a teacher longs to hear. Here, then, in brief, is the method of meditation I teach. (There are full instructions in my book *Meditation,* along with descriptions of seven other points to observe for supporting your meditation during the day.)

★ Choose – or make, if you have to – a time for meditation when you can sit for half an hour in uninterrupted quiet. Early morning is best. If you wish to meditate more, add half an hour in the evening, but please do not meditate for longer periods without personal guidance from an experienced teacher.

★ Select a place that is cool, clean, and quiet. Sit with your back and head erect, on the floor or on a straight-backed chair.

★ Close your eyes and begin to go *slowly,* in your mind, through the words of a simple, positive, inspirational passage from one of the world's great spiritual traditions. (Remember, you become what you meditate on.) I recommend beginning with the Prayer of Saint Francis of Assisi:

> Lord, make me an instrument of thy peace.
> Where there is hatred, let me sow love;
> Where there is injury, pardon;
> Where there is doubt, faith;
> Where there is despair, hope;
> Where there is darkness, light;
> Where there is sadness, joy.
>
> O divine Master, grant that I may not so much seek
> To be consoled as to console,
> To be understood as to understand,
> To be loved as to love;
> For it is in giving that we receive;
> It is in pardoning that we are pardoned;
> It is in dying [to self] that we are born to eternal life.

You will find it helpful to keep adding to your repertoire so that the passages you meditate on do not grow stale. My book *God Makes the Rivers to Flow* contains other passages that I recommend, drawn from many traditions. But whatever your background, I suggest you begin by giving Saint Francis a try. You will find that his words are both personal and universal and that they have great power to heal old wounds deep in the mind. If words like "Lord" bother you, remind yourself that you are addressing the divine spark within your own heart: not some imposing figure seated on a throne in the far reaches of the heavens, but the very core of your own self.

★ While you are meditating, do not follow any association of ideas or allow your mind to reflect on the meaning of the words. If you are giving your full attention to each word, the meaning cannot help sinking in.

★ When distractions come, do not resist them, but give more attention to the words of the passage. If your mind strays from the passage entirely, bring it back gently to the beginning and start again.

★ Resolve to have your meditation every day – however full your schedule, whatever interruptions threaten, whether you are sick or well. If you miss one day, goes an old Hindu saying, you will need seven days to make it up.

Meditation is simple, but it is far from easy. One friend asked me recently why I call the Beatitudes "strategies." Isn't the word borrowed from war? It is. But the spiritual life too is a battle. Mystics call it the war within: the conflict between what is spiritual in us and what is selfish, between the force of goodness and the powers of destruction that clash incessantly in every human heart.

"There is no greater valor nor no sterner fight," attests Eckhart. As always, Eckhart is terse and to the point: because "he who would be what he ought to be must stop being what he is." That is the challenge of the spiritual life – and that challenge is part of its appeal. It is precisely because the quest to realize God is so difficult that those who are really daring – and there are many in this country – should be eager to take it up. In fact, the mystics say, all the daring and aggressiveness in human nature are given to us for one supreme evolutionary purpose: to remove what covers our original goodness so that we can reveal more and more of God in our own lives.

To that end, we can take up the Beatitudes one by one as strategies for winning the war within.

CHAPTER 2
Purity

Blessed are the pure in heart, for they shall see God.

WHEN I WAS A BOY, growing up in a village in South India, just an hour's walk from my home was a dense jungle where wild animals roamed at will. Often I used to thrill to the trumpeting of an elephant, and rumors abounded among the children that tigers strayed from the jungle at night and prowled the village paths. You can imagine some of the nightmares I had as a child, dreaming that a tiger had crept into my room and was padding noiselessly toward my bed . . .

Suppose, now, that at just such a moment of terror you could somehow have entered my dream – just as you are, wide awake. "Wake up, Easwaran! There's no tiger. You're just dreaming, safe in your own bed."

Still asleep, I would think you were part of my dream. "What do you mean, there's no tiger? I can see it with my own eyes. I can smell it and feel its hot breath on my face. If you don't believe me, see how my pulse is racing. Feel my forehead; it's wet with the dew of fear. My whole body is flooded with adrenaline for fight or flight . . . preferably flight! All the evidence of my senses tells me that tiger is real, and if you're not going to do anything to help me, you might as well not have come."

At that point, you might grab me by the shoulders and shake me awake. Only then would I look around and say sheepishly, "Oh, yes, it *was* a dream. My heart is still pounding, but I can see there never was a tiger at all."

We are used to calling dreams unreal, but that is not entirely accurate. How do we decide that the world of our senses is real? Dream experience can be full of sensory detail, and as far as the nervous system is concerned, those sensations are the same as those of waking life. We can see, feel, taste, smell, or hear things in a dream so vividly that the body actually responds with the chemistry of desire, anger, or fear. Even after we wake up, the illusion of reality may remain. And when nothing is left but the memory, how much difference is there between a waking experience and a dream?

"Dreams are real as long as they last," the psychologist Havelock Ellis once observed. "Can we say more of life?" It is a provocative question, and one which the mystics ask as well, but from a different perspective. When we wake up from a dream, they say, we do not pass from unreality to reality; we pass from a lower level of reality to a higher level. And, they add, there is a higher level still, compared with which this waking life of ours is as insubstantial as a dream.

To put it more bluntly, we are living in our sleep, dreaming that things like money and pleasure can make us happy. When they do not, it's a nightmare. When you read the Beatitudes, think of Jesus entering our dream world and showing us how we can wake up, just as from a dream, into a higher reality: the kingdom of heaven here on earth.

Yet until we do wake up, nothing sounds more absurd

than the assertion that we are dreaming – and nothing seems more solid than this world of the senses. Why should this be so? If original goodness is our real nature, why are we unable to see it?

The mystics' answer is simple: because we see life not as it is but as we are. We see "through a glass darkly," through the distorting lenses of the mind – all the layers of feeling, habit, instinct, and memory that cover the pure core of goodness deep within.

To explain this, Christian mystics have drawn a comparison with a glass lantern clouded with oil and soot. To see the light, we have to clean the panes. In modern terms, the panes are the mind: the layers of consciousness that make up our personality.

As we might expect, Eckhart uses even more vigorous language. There are many of these layers, he tells us, each doing its part to hide from us who we really are:

A human being has so many skins inside, covering
the depths of the heart. We know so many things, but
we don't know ourselves! Why, thirty or forty skins
or hides, as thick and hard as an ox's or a bear's, cover
the soul. Go into your own ground and learn to know
yourself there.

One of the easiest ways to understand how the mind itself distorts the way we see is to take a closer look at sensory perception. We like to think of sight, sound, touch, smell, and taste as direct encounters with the real world, but that is not really accurate. What we actually encounter are the images we form from the electrochemical data the senses supply to the brain. In other words, we see not so much with the eyes as with the mind, for it is the mind that arranges and interprets the information of the senses according to its own conditioning. "Hard" and "round," "red" and "green" are not qualities in the world outside; they are concepts. Even a kitchen table is a *table* only in the mind.

Today the "new physics" is a popular topic. Almost everyone is prepared to consider the proposal that physical objects are not necessarily what they seem. For example, the desk at which I am writing is not really solid; it *appears* solid because of the limitations of my instruments of observation. If human beings were sentient clouds of X rays, we would not call a desk solid; we would be able to walk right through it. Lead would be solid, but wood would be part of the atmosphere. And if our eyes registered radio waves instead of what we call visible light, we would not see a desk at all. My study might look like a kind of beach, awash with the flotsam of rock music broadcasts and the evening news.

Similarly, there is no red carpet here beneath my feet, although I would attest confidently that there is – and so would you if you were here. There is an object which we agree to call "carpet," yet there is no redness in it; the redness is in my mind. To our black cat, Luther, who regards my study as his, everything would be what we humans call gray; or, more precisely, things would have no color at all. In Luther's feline world there might be no object "floor" as distinct from "carpet," only "warm space" and "unpleasantly cold." Color, and all the other qualities that make a thing what it is, depend on the particular modes of perception given us by our five senses.

Nothing in the external world, then, really *is* what we see. (We might press the point and say that we never really encounter the external world at all.) This is a sobering realization, so we can be glad that no one takes it too seriously. For matters of convenience, we all accept what we know to be a faulty position: that what we see is what is there, and that each of us sees the same world.

I want to make it clear that when the mystics talk about layers of consciousness, they are not talking theory. They are describing regions of experience so nearly palpable that each one has an almost optical effect on the way we see life. The world within has vast domains which, though we never consciously visit them, shape our perception, understanding, and behavior.

This is not a merely mystical notion. "Our normal, waking consciousness," says the brilliant American psychologist William James,

> rational consciousness as we call it, is but one special type of consciousness; whilst all about it, parted from it by the filmiest of screens, there lie potential forms of consciousness entirely different.

This is no mystic speaking; this is a hardheaded scientist, virtually the father of the pragmatic school of psychology, speaking from his own experience. While you are sitting there in your chair reading, he says, vast regions of personality lie open in the world within: the force fields of the unconscious, which shape our thought and action. "We may go through life without suspecting their existence," James continues,

> but apply the requisite stimulus, and at a touch they are there in all their completeness, definite types of mentality which probably somewhere have their field of application and adaptation. No account of the universe in its totality can be final which leaves these other forms of consciousness quite disregarded. How to regard them is the question, – for they are so discontinuous with ordinary consciousness. Yet they may determine attitudes although they cannot furnish formulas, and open a region though they fail to give a map. At any rate, they forbid a premature closing of our accounts with reality.

"How to regard them is the question": that is, how to see them, how to study and know and master them. That is the purpose of meditation. "Looking back on my own experiences" of these deeper states, James continues, "they all converge towards a kind of insight. . . . The keynote of it is invariably a reconciliation. It is as if the opposites of the world, whose contradictoriness and conflict make all our difficulties and troubles, were melted into unity."

Contemporary physicists sometimes say that instead of the observable universe of classical physics, they have to deal with a "participatory universe" in which, at least on a subatomic level, the act of observation participates in the result. The mystics say something similar but even farther reaching: each of us lives in a truly participatory universe of his or her own making.

This is difficult to grasp. We can accept that the senses, although useful, do not report life as it really is; but to be told that the mind, too, while useful, is a distorting medium – that is more than most of us will buy. At least where the senses are concerned, we are generally in agreement: this desk *is* solid, whatever physicists may say. But where the mind is concerned, consensus is out. All of us have our own individual perceptions.

To begin with, it is our mental apparatus – our feelings, memories, and desires – that selects what we even perceive. Out of the vast confusion of data that our senses present, it is the mind that decides what registers. Anything that fails to fit our interests or understanding is not introduced to our attention. What we see – and therefore the world we live in, *our* world as opposed to others' – is a function of our own thinking.

Have you ever had the experience of hearing one acquaintance described by another and wondering to yourself, "Is that really the same man?" Or perhaps you and a friend stray for the first time onto sensitive ground, some question of politics or race or religion, and you think, "I've never really seen that person before!" And in matters of the heart, everyone knows how infatuation can fool us, though at the time that is how we actually see. While the flames of desire are high, ask a Romeo to describe his Juliet. "So gentle, so thoughtful, always ready with something nice to say." Ask him again when the relationship is over; you may think he is talking about a different person.

More accurately, *he* is a different person. That is why his perceptions have changed. "I just didn't see clearly then," he would say. "Now I know what she's really like." But that is neither true nor fair. Before, Romeo saw Juliet with the eyes of desire; now, that desire is gone and he sees different things. Both perceptions have truth in them and falsehood, and neither view is whole. What we see is a function of what we desire.

It is in the mind that we experience life, and the mind is never really clear. You know that when your mind is angry, its findings are not reliable; you see things differently when it quiets down. When your mind is afraid, its view is faulty; you find things to be afraid of everywhere. And when your mind is surging with a strong desire, you see everything in terms of satisfying that desire – which raises a big question mark over anything the mind tells you to do.

And below these relatively superficial levels, beneath the emotions we are ordinarily aware of, lie layer on layer of the unconscious mind. These are the depths an unknown fourteenth-century mystic called vividly the "cloud of unknowing," where primordial instincts, fears, and urges cover our understanding so that we see nothing except ourselves.

The deepest flaw in the mind is what Einstein called the "kind of optical delusion of consciousness" that makes us see ourselves as separate from the rest of life. In my interpretation of the metaphor of Eden in the previous chapter, this fundamental fracture in consciousness is the I-sense, the Big Bang that triggers our Fall into separateness. Like a crack in glasses that we must wear every moment of our lives, this division is built into the mind. "I" versus "not-I" runs through everything we see.

Imagine if some genius invented a set of binoculars with conflicting lenses, so that each eye saw things differently from the other. It would confuse you completely. You would go after something or someone and trip over things you did not even see, then get up wondering why you fell. "Why is life so unfair?" Isn't that how it is? In the same way, the mystics say, we are looking at the world – all of us – through two conflicting lenses at the same time, one of which sees only "I, I, I" and the other "Not me! Not mine!" In practical terms, it means we see life divided in every way: my needs as opposed to yours, my family as opposed to yours; my country and not yours, my race, my religion . . . "I am right, so you must be wrong"; "What I like is good, so what I don't like must be bad": the refrain goes on and on.

To see life as it is, all these refracting influences have to be removed so that consciousness is pure and clear. "If the doors of perception were cleansed," as Blake said in famous lines, "everything would be seen as it is, infinite."

"Blessed are the pure in heart, for they shall see God." Jesus is not being rhetorical. He is describing in simple language what the realization of God means. When the distorting instrument of the mind is made clear, we see life not as a collection of fragments but as a seamless whole. We see the divine spark at the center of our very being; and we see simultaneously that in the heart of every other human being – in every country, of every race – though hidden perhaps by clouds of ignorance and conditioning, that same spark is present, one and the same in all. The Flemish mystic Ruysroeck explains:

> The image of God is found *essentially* and *personally* in all. Each of us possesses it whole, entire and undivided, and all of us together [do] not [possess it] more than one person does alone. In this way we are all one, intimately united in our eternal image, which is the image of God. . . .

Blake's words about the "doors of perception," of course, are familiar to us today largely because of Huxley's experiments with mescaline, which encouraged so many young people to play with hallucinogens in the sixties. Today, almost a generation later, I think most thoughtful people understand that drugs never "cleanse" the senses; they only cloud the mind, adding one level of unreality over another. It is the mind that must be made pure, and that means that everything that distorts it must be quieted or removed.

In mysticism the mind is often compared to a lake, whose waters become clouded with mud when the lake is agitated. Only when the murk of our thoughts, desires, and passions settles does the mind become calm and clear. When the mind is completely still, the mystics say, unstirred even in its depths, we see straight through to the ground of our being, which is divine. On this, the mystics of all religions are in agreement. "Be still," says the Lord, "and know that I am God." And the Upanishads, the purest source of the Perennial Philosophy in the world, add:

> When the five senses are stilled, when the mind is stilled,
> when the intellect is stilled, that is called the highest state
> by the wise. They say yoga is this complete stillness in
> which one enters the unitive state, never to become separate again.

When we finally wake up from this long, lurid dream of separate existence, the mystics tell us, we will just rub our eyes; we will not believe how we used to see. The illusion of separateness will be gone, and we will see life as one indivisible whole: men, women, and children, "the beasts of the field and the birds of the air," all the created universe. This is not just intellectual knowledge or poetic vision. The vision of unity transforms our life from the inside out. In that moment of transcendental insight, says Ruysbroeck, we are wrought and transformed . . . and as the air is penetrated by the sun, thus we receive in quietude of spirit the Incomprehensible Light, enfolding us and penetrating us. And this Light is nothing else but an infinite gazing and seeing. We behold that which we are, and we are that which we behold; because our thought, life and being are uplifted in simplicity and made one with the Truth which is God.

"We behold that which we are, and we are that which we behold." Perfect words. "As a man is, so he sees," Blake once wrote to a critic:

I see everything I paint in this world, but everybody does not see alike. To the eye of a miser a guinea is far more beautiful than the sun, and a bag worn with the use of money has more beautiful proportions than a vine filled with grapes. The tree which moves some to tears of joy is in the eyes of others only a green thing which stands in the way. . . . But to the eyes of the man of imagination, Nature is Imagination itself.

Similarly, to the eyes of the man or woman of God, nature is God himself. So Angela of Foligno, a Franciscan just one generation after Francis and a contemporary of Eckhart's, exclaims in one of the most quoted passages in Christian mysticism:

The eyes of my soul were opened, and I beheld the plenitude of God, wherein I did comprehend the whole world, both here and beyond the sea, and the abyss and ocean and all things. In all these things I beheld naught save the divine power, in a manner assuredly indescribable; so that through excess of marveling the soul cried with a loud voice, saying "This whole world is full of God!"

Sometimes this revelation comes in one swift, wordless opening into eternity, as happened to Juliana of Norwich:

. . . He showed me a little thing, the quality of an hazelnut in the palm of my hand; and it was round as a ball. I looked thereupon with the eye of my understanding, and thought: What may this be? And it was answered generally thus: It is all that is made. And I marveled how it might last, for methought it might suddenly have fallen to naught for littleness. And I was answered in my understanding: It lasteth and ever shall last, for that God loveth it. And so All-Thing hath Being by the love of God.

Or it may come less dramatically, though with equal authority, in a quiet moment of insight that transforms one's life completely – as happened at the age of eighteen to Brother Lawrence, a simple lay brother of the Carmelite order in seventeenth-century France. An anonymous chronicler describes Brother Lawrence's experience:

> In the winter, seeing a tree stripped of its leaves, and considering that within a little time the leaves would be renewed, and after that the flowers and fruit appear, he received a high view of the providence and power of God which has never since been effaced from his soul. . . . This view had set him perfectly loose from the world and kindled in him such a love for God that he could not tell whether it had increased in the more than forty years that he had lived since.

Can we expect, then, to spend Friday afternoons in the park gazing at hydrangeas and one day walk home full of wisdom? Probably not. Insights of this order do not really come as a bolt out of the blue. The unitive visions of Angela, Juliana, and Brother Lawrence must have been prepared for deep within their hearts, surging to the surface when the time was ripe for the veil to be torn away. In traditional language, they had already made themselves pure in heart. How many young men had passed that same stripped tree and seen nothing but bare branches? But within the one particular teenager who would become

Brother Lawrence, a realization was stirring to life; the tree was merely a catalyst.

"If your heart were sincere and upright," says Thomas a Kempis, "every creature would be unto you a looking-glass of life and a book of holy doctrine." The pure in spirit, who see God, see him here and now: in his handiwork, his hidden purpose, the wry humor of his creation. "Heaven lies about us in our infancy," wrote Wordsworth, and in that sense the mystic is always a child.

The Lord has left us love notes, wondrous *billets-doux*, scattered extravagantly across creation. Hidden in the eye of the tiger, the wet muzzle of a calf, the delicacy of the violet, and the perfect curve of the elephant's tusk is a very personal, priceless message: "God is love, and he who abides in love abides in God, and God in him."

Watch the lamb in awkward play, butting against its mother's side. See the spider putting the final shimmering touches on an architectural wonder. And absorb a truth that is wordless. The grace of a deer, the soaring freedom of a sparrow hawk in flight, the utter self-possession of an elephant crashing through the woods – in every one of these there is something of ourselves. From the great whales to the tiniest of tree frogs in the Amazon basin, unity embraces us all. Lose sight of this unity, allow these creatures to be exploited or destroyed, and we are diminished too.

*

Friends often tell me, "But I can't make myself pure! I have very negative thoughts. A person like you wouldn't understand just how negative!" I assure them that indeed I do understand. How many are born pure in heart? Yet in all the major religions, superb teachers have given clear instructions in how to make our minds pure so that divinity can shine forth: how to transform our personality from self-centered to selfless, from unconcerned to caring, eventually even from human to divine.

Intellectual study cannot be of much help in this transformation. Only meditation, the systematic turning inward of attention, can take us deep into consciousness where the obstacles to a pure heart hide.

From this point of view, meditation can be described as nothing more or less than the purification of consciousness, by removing everything that obstructs our vision of the divine core in others and in ourselves. This process is described in a remarkable mystical document of thirteenth-century Europe called *Cleaving to God,* attributed to a great predecessor of Eckhart's known as Albertus Magnus:

> We must cast out of our minds the impressions and images and forms of all things which are not God so that we may look upon God within our own soul; for the soul is more intimately and more closely present to each thing than each thing is to itself. When we enter deeply into ourselves, the eye of inner vision is opened and a ladder is prepared by which the soul may ascend to the contemplation of God.

For myself, however, I prefer a more positive way to explain how meditation works: not as trying to "empty the mind," which is misleading, but as trying to *still* the mind, by bringing all its turbulent activity to acute focus on a single point.

In meditation, when you go through an inspirational passage such as the Prayer of Saint Francis with complete attention, each significant word or phrase drops like a jewel into the depths of consciousness. With each sentence you are absorbing the loftiest image of human nature. When your absorption in the passage is complete, nothing else will remain in your consciousness. Saint Francis's ideals will gradually displace all negative thoughts, so that little by little, divinity begins to shine through. Your mind *is* empty of yourself, true; but that is also to say it is full of God.

This may sound simple, but it is far from easy. Ask the mystics themselves: they will tell you how hard it is to get deep beneath the surface of the mind and remove everything that is not in harmony with the core of divinity within. The miracle is that it can be done at all. In spite of how the horizons of knowledge keep expanding, the one thing almost no one even suspects today is that it is actually possible, with a good deal of effort, to penetrate the depths of the unconscious mind and bring about the kind of unifying changes which will make a new person of us. This is the best-kept secret of the ages: that any one of us can become the kind of person he or she dreams of becoming.

Meister Eckhart calls this process "the pauper becoming the prince." Of which kingdom? The most important in the world: the realm of our own thoughts, over which very, very few of us can claim to have authority. This sovereignty confers real power, much more significant than the might of kings; for everything of value comes from the way we think. That is the power that meditation can put into our hands.

"I have not the slightest doubt," Mahatma Gandhi said, "that prayer is an unfailing means of cleansing the heart of passions." The same is true of meditation. Gandhi was a lawyer, you know, and very finicky about his words. He never put anything into print that was not true in his own experience. "But," he adds, "it must combine with the utmost humility. Prayer is an impossibility without a living faith in the presence of God within" – that is, without faith in the core of goodness in others and in ourselves. We have to be patient with ourselves, Gandhi is reminding us, and not demand miracles overnight. Always keep in mind that this center of purity *is* there, however unlikely that may seem, and keep on trying to uncover it. Whether the results are seen by us or not, every bit of effort helps.

I want to repeat: even some of the greatest of spiritual figures had a lot of work to do to make their consciousness pure enough for divinity to shine through. When someone treats you unfairly or unkindly, it is only natural for your mind to be flooded with resentment; everybody's mind works that way. But the day can come when you scarcely remember what resentment means. It is not that you will be blind to others' behavior, but that negative responses will not even arise in your mind: and when negative thoughts do not arise, you respond to every situation with love. This is what it means to be "pure in heart." No one should expect total freedom from negative emotions, but this innocence of heart is something we can aim at every day.

Besides meditation, there is another powerful tool for purifying consciousness that can be used at almost any time during the day. Meditation is a demanding discipline, but even children can learn to use what in Sanskrit is called the *mantram.*

The mantram, or Holy Name, is a short, potent spiritual formula for the highest that we can conceive, and it is found in the annals of every major religion. According to tradition, the earliest Christian communities used some form of the Prayer of Jesus – simply the name of Jesus, or a variation like *Lord, Jesus Christ, Son of God, have mercy* – in precisely the same way as Mahatma Gandhi repeated *Rama, Rama,* or as Jewish mystics have repeated the Shema or *Ribono shel olam,* "Lord of the universe."

You will find full instructions for using the mantram in my little book *The Mantram Handbook,* but briefly, the mantram can be repeated silently in your mind whenever your mind is running off at the mouth – which for all of us is likely to be much more often than we suspect. Instead of worrying, fussing, fretting, fuming, steaming, simmering, daydreaming, or woolgathering, repeat the mantram. Nothing will be lost, and you will find that every repetition helps to steady your mind and sharpen your appreciation of life around you.

I wish I could share with every person in this country what repeating the name of the Lord can do. It "restoreth the soul," in David's beautiful phrase, as you will see for yourself if you give it a try. It brings energy, security, and self-confidence, and, especially in the turmoil of the teen years, there is probably no skill of greater value.

The Lord's Prayer begins, "hallowed be thy name." How do we hallow the name of the Lord? By driving it deep into the mind until it becomes a kind of channel into deepest consciousness, through which we can draw increasing reserves of patience, love, insight, and understanding.

This does require determination, I admit. I used to hunt through my days for opportunities to repeat the Holy Name, scavenging leisure moments like those curious characters who dowse for buried treasures at the beach, scanning every inch of sand with a metal detector at the end of a long wand. It calls for a great deal of patience, but the effort pays off. Today, because of all that effort, I no longer have to make myself repeat the Holy Name. It repeats itself, warding off every negative state of mind.

From the *Cloud of Unknowing,* written by an anonymous English mystic in the second half of the fourteenth century, comes one of the most stirring pieces of instruction I have seen on the protective power of the Holy Name:

> And if thou desirest to have this intent lapped and folden in one word, so that thou mayest have better hold thereupon, take thee but a little word. . . .
> The word shall be thy shield and thy spear, whether

thou ridest on peace or on war. With this word thou
shalt beat on this cloud and this darkness above thee.
With this word thou shalt smite down all manner of
thought under the *cloud of forgetting.* Insomuch that, if
any thought press upon thee to ask what thou wouldst
have, answer with no more words than with this one
word. . . . And if thou wilt hold fast to this purpose,
be sure that that thought will no while bide.

Translate that into contemporary terms and you will
understand why the mantram is so effective in dealing
with addictive habits and compulsive behavior. Whenever
the mind starts to clamor for something you do not ap-
prove, this unknown mystic says, repeat the mantram.
When your attention gets hold of the mantram, it is off the
compulsion; then you are free again to think and act as
you choose.

Again, in modern terms, this "cloud of unknowing" is
the unconscious. When the Holy Name is established in
these depths, it brings choice and the will into areas ordinarily beyond human reach. Eventually the mantram
will be constantly on alert. It will hide behind the bushes
of your mind like a Highway Patrol cruiser, waiting to
nab any speeding thoughts and intoxicated desires that
start weaving out onto the road. Even at night, in your
dreams, the mantram will block unsavory thoughts that
are trying to sneak in unnoticed. This vigilance is what
Brother Lawrence called "practicing the presence of
God." Those who are established in this presence, Eckhart said, carry God with them wherever they go.

Like meditation, repetition of the Holy Name can be
thought of as a way of communicating with the Lord
within. But it is much less formal. Meditation is something you do at a certain time and place every day, always
following the instructions carefully. But you can repeat
the mantram at almost any time, whenever your mind is
agitated or idle.

★

It must be admitted that the active life and the contemplative life do appear at times to exclude one another. But on the other hand, we have the assurance and the example of deeply committed men and women of God that the two actually require each other. Meister Eckhart says explicitly, "What a man takes in by contemplation, that he pours out in love."

Saint Teresa of Avila and Saint John of the Cross, two of the greatest figures in world mysticism, carried on a kind of lover's quarrel on this point for many years. Teresa, a master of interior prayer and a brilliantly practical teacher, was also one of the world's greatest activists, constantly harassed by difficulties in founding and strengthening the convents of her Sisters of Carmel. And John was a born contemplative whose deeply interior life scarcely touched the earth except when he paused to set down some of the most lyrical poems in Spanish literature. As Teresa's confessor, he kept urging her to conserve her strength and indulge her genius for meditation, leaving to others the business of household accounts and quarrels within her convents. Yet how could she not stir herself when there was work to do, and when she felt the call was coming from her Lord himself? So the tender wrangling went on, up until her last days.

After Teresa slipped from this world, it astonished those close to her to see John, devoted until then to a life of seclusion and prayer, throwing himself heart and soul into the work she had had to leave. Yet there were some who saw no contradiction; as Ruysbroeck had pointed out two centuries before, "love would ever be active: for its nature is eternal working with God." The love released in the unitive vision fuses contemplation and action, meditation and selfless service:

[God] demands of us both action and fruition, in such
a way that the action never hinders the fruition, nor the
fruition the action, but they strengthen one another.
. . . [Thus such a person] dwells in God; and yet he
goes out towards all creatures, in a spirit of love towards
all things, in virtue and in works of righteousness. *And
this is the supreme summit of the inner life.*

★

If we were "inwardly good and pure," says Thomas a
Kempis, we would be able to "see and understand all
things well without impediment." When the heart is
pure, nothing stands between ourselves and God within.

When I began teaching English, at a college in Central
India, I had many Muslim students in my class. The
young men sat on one side of the room, and the girls, hidden behind veils, sat on the other. The boys I could see, of
course – their high foreheads, aquiline noses, and deter-
mined chins, characteristic of the old Muslim families of
that area. But the girls' faces I could not see at all. How
was I to tell whether my learned orations on *Othello* and
Hamlet made any sense behind those veils? For an en-
thusiastic new teacher, it was a frustrating situation.

I went to my Muslim colleagues on the staff. "What do
you do?" I asked. "I can't see the girls' faces, so I can't tell
if I'm getting through to them."

My friends smiled. "We're used to it," one of them said,
"so we've learned to sharpen our eyes. To us, the veil is
not nearly so concealing as it seems. Focus your attention
and you'll find you can see much more than you think."

He gave me some pointers, and with practice I found
that I could catch the rustle of silk that hid a smile, tell
from which young lady a particular giggle was coming.
Before long I felt completely at home.

Against this kind of background, the mystics of Islam
describe God as hidden by seven veils, each a particular

layer of consciousness. As meditation deepens, we begin to see through these veils more and more clearly. The dazzling diversity at the surface of life gradually loses its power to distract and confuse us. Finally, in the tremendous climax of meditation which Indian mysticism calls *samadhi,* we actually pierce the veil of multiplicity and change. Then we see, at the very heart of existence, a reality that abides: "uncreated and uncreatable . . . which neither space nor time touches."

This kind of intense concentration is always required to see order and meaning in the world around us. Scientists find laws in the apparent confusion of sense experience in very much the same way. From the outset they operate on the firm faith that a meaningful pattern does exist, and that faith focuses their attention and their training. With unified vision they seize upon patterns that hold true against all tests.

The mystics too are certain that life makes sense. They too set out, as the British biologist Sir Peter Medawar puts it, fired with the "rage to *know.*" Nothing will do until they have penetrated the unity they know must lie at the heart of life. And when they begin to understand what the Sufis say – "You yourself are the veil that stands between you and God" – there arises a burning desire to get everything petty and selfish in that small self out of the way. But we start out, as a scientist does, with that first provisional faith that meaning *is* there to be found. "This is the reason," Augustine says, "that we trust what we are to believe before we see it: that by believing we may purify the heart, whereby we may be able to see."

But what actually focuses our vision? In a word, desire: the ardent passion to see and understand. What we are asked to do is just what Jesus and Moses emphasized in ringing words: "Thou shalt love thy God with all thy heart and with all thy soul." *Then* we shall see him: not with our eyes, Eckhart says, "as one sees a cow," but as a living presence in every creature.

No one begins like this. We start out with a lot of desires for many things, and when we hear Jesus' injunction, the reply that our lives give is, "Of course, Lord! There *are* some attachments to other things – my sauna, my van, my new sound system and Nautilus machine. But whatever love is left after that, I'll gladly give to you." And the Lord says patiently, "Why don't you keep that too? I'm prepared to wait."

Blessed are the pure in heart. We are used to thinking of purity in terms of cleansing, but in practice this unification of desires is the key. "Purity of heart," says Kierkegaard, "is to will one thing." As meditation deepens, the desire to go even deeper slowly absorbs all kinds of lesser desires. Activities that are less important to us begin to fall away. But those desires do not really disappear. Their power is simply drawn up into a deeper current, the longing of the soul for fulfillment.

Hidden inside, all of us carry a purifying fire. It may be banked with ashes that seem cold to the touch, but a spark of the divine is there nonetheless, ready to leap into life. This "hidden fire," as William Law called it, is nothing less than love of God. It is latent in every one of us, even the most jaded, the most disillusioned, the most embittered, because that spark is the one part of us that we can never lose. It wants surprisingly little encouragement to flare into vibrant life and shed light and warmth all around.

The rest of the Beatitudes tell us how this is to be done.

CHAPTER 3
Humility

Blessed are the poor in spirit, for theirs is the kingdom of heaven.

WHEN I FIRST came to this country, I was invited to give a series of talks on meditation and mysticism in San Francisco. I was interested to find several confirmed beatniks in my audience. They didn't think much of traditional religious language, and they didn't like mincing words; when they disagreed with me, they said so straight. One evening, without intending to, I shocked them by quoting a passage referring to heaven and hell.

"You're such an educated, cultured person," a friend objected afterward in dismay. "How can you believe in these medieval ideas?"

"To tell the truth," I answered, "I don't really think they're medieval. I have seen quite a few people actually living in hell – and one or two in heaven." Whenever we get swept away by a selfish urge or a wave of anger, we are in hell; we can almost feel the sulfurous fumes of insecurity and fear. If we get so angry that we can't sleep, we are overnight guests in hell's hotel.

"Well, that's different," my friend replied in relief. "Now you're just being metaphorical. I thought you really believed it."

"Hell is no metaphor," I said, "and neither is heaven. Hell and heaven are states of consciousness. Doesn't Jesus say the kingdom of heaven is within? And mental states are real – in fact, in some ways they are even more 'thingy' than things. If I were to throw this pen at you, you might get a little bruise. But if I said something unkind and you couldn't stop thinking about it, your resentment might burn for years. It might even aggravate your ulcer."

"I thought you were talking about sin," he said a little grumpily. "I just don't hold with those old ideas about sin and punishment."

"I don't usually talk about sin," I admitted: "not because it's not real, but because when you go on saying 'I'm a sinner, I'm a sinner,' you're actually thinking of yourself as a sinner. You expect yourself to do wrong things, so you're that much more likely to go on doing them. I like to emphasize original goodness: 'I'm a saint, I'm a saint – *potentially.*'

"But," I added, "my real objection to those 'old ideas' is that they make it sound as if punishment is heaped on our heads by some wrathful God outside us. Heaven and hell are *inside.* We don't have to have somebody punish us for doing wrong; we punish ourselves. Sin is its own punishment."

This approach appeals to me deeply, and since those early days I have found that it makes good sense to a modern audience too. It is not really a new idea – Christian writers since the Desert Fathers have spoken clearly of these things, and no one is more precise on the subject than the Buddha. But today it appeals to our scientific temper. We do not have to be punished for getting angry, for example; anger is its own punishment. The next time someone flies into a rage before you, watch objectively and you will see what it does to the body, pumping up blood pressure, flooding vital organs and tissues with adrenaline, and subjecting the body to all kinds of physiologic stress. When I see someone getting angry, I think to myself, "That's a thousandth of a heart attack!" These things add up, and people have actually died of a cardiovascular accident brought on by the thousandth burst of rage.

More subtly, dwelling on yourself is its own punishment. All of us find ourselves a fascinating, satisfying subject to contemplate . . . until the results begin to accumulate. The effects are easier to see with someone else: the person who thinks about himself all the time, who can scarcely think about anything except in connection with his own needs, becomes the most wretched creature on earth. Nothing really goes the way he wants, and that preoccupation with himself that seemed so pleasant and natural becomes a wall that keeps everyone else outside. It's a lonely, tormented life. Perhaps the most painful irony is that this wretchedness too is just dwelling on oneself. Once the habit is formed, the mind cannot stop, even when it makes us miserable.

Here spiritual psychology cuts to the heart of the matter in one incisive stroke. All these habits of mind that can make life hell, the mystics say, can be traced to one central flaw of attention. To call it self-preoccupation comes close: the habit of dwelling on *my* needs, *my* desires, *my* plans, *my* fears. The more deeply ingrained this pattern of thinking is, the mystics say, the more we make ourselves a little island isolated from the rest of life, with all the unhappiness that has to follow. This is not a moral judgment; it is simply the way happiness works. Asking life to make a selfish person happy, my grandmother used to say, is like asking a banana tree to give you mangoes.

But there is a better word for this habit of mind: self-will, the insistent drive to have our own way, to get what we want, whatever it may cost. Self-will has a million forms, but every one of them is a kind of torment. Whenever we feel life is being unfair to us, whenever we hurt because people are not treating us right or paying us attention or giving us our due respect, nine times out of ten what is hurting is our self-will. An anonymous mystical document known as the *Theologica Germanica* says succinctly, "Nothing burns in hell except self-will." No God has to punish us for being self-willed; self-will is its own punishment, its own hell.

"Blessed are the poor in spirit, for theirs is the kingdom of heaven." The meaning of the Biblical phrase here is not "poor-spirited." It is just the opposite of being full of ourselves – that is, just the opposite of being full of self-will. When we are in the grips of self-will, life cannot help stepping on our toes, and we cannot help being thrown into turmoil when things do not go our way.

On the other hand, in those moments when we forget ourselves – not thinking "Am I happy? Am I having fun yet?" but completely oblivious to our little ego – we spend a brief but beautiful holiday in heaven.

The mystics tell us that the joy we experience in these moments of self-forgetting is our true nature, our native state. To regain it, we have simply to empty ourselves of what hides this joy: that is, to stop dwelling on ourselves. To the extent that we are not full of ourselves, God can fill us – in fact, the mystics say daringly, he *has* to. "When we thus clear the ground and make our soul ready," says John Tauler, a pupil of Eckhart's and a brilliant mystic in his own right,

> without doubt God must fill up the void. . . . If you go out of yourself, without doubt he shall go in, and there will be much or little of his entering in according to how much or little you go out.

And Eckhart adds, in his wonderfully pungent way: "God expects but one thing of you, and that is that you should come out of yourself in so far as you are a created being and let God be God in you."

How far modern civilization has gone to the other extreme! Self-will has always been human nature, but today it is almost worshipped in some circles. Unselfishness is considered old-fashioned and unnatural, and to be happy, some professional psychologists say, we have to learn to assert ourselves, attend to our personal needs first, "look out for number one."

To be sure, there are reasons for these extreme positions. People think that being unselfish is boring, that a selfless person cannot possibly enjoy life because he is constantly making himself a doormat, that to have a high sense of worth you have to have a big ego. These are just misunderstandings, but the observation remains true: our age sets a premium on self-will in aggressiveness, competitiveness, and self-aggrandizement; that, we are told, is the route to joy.

Yet to live as a separate creature, cut off from the rest of life, is just the opposite of joy. The Persian mystic Jalaluddin Rumi summed up the spiritual quest in one quiet sentence: "Pilgrimage to the place of the wise is to find escape from the flame of separateness." Ultimately, self-will becomes a solid wall that keeps others out and ourselves walled in. Imagine trying to walk around the Great Wall of China, fourteen hundred miles of meandering masonry clinging to every hill and valley as far as the eye can see. That is what trying to get around self-will is like. When we feel intense anguish in a personal relationship, more often than not what pains us is not differences of politics or taste; it is just self-will in another of its disguises, hurting because it cannot have its way.

I like to think of self-will as love turned around. Love is

energy, and self-will is that energy focused on oneself. We can learn to free that energy, and when we do, our lives will fill with love – which is what living in heaven means.

In today's competitive climate, often those who are aggressive about imposing their will on others are labeled "successful." But the accomplishments of such people are often sadly short-lived, while the damage they do themselves and others can be far-reaching. When self-will is excessive, we end up offending others, feeling offended, and lashing back, and that undoes everything worthwhile we might achieve.

People with little self-will, on the other hand, seldom get upset when life goes against them. They do not try to impose their way on others, or get agitated or depressed or defensive when people hold different views. Being intolerant of other views, Mahatma Gandhi used to say, is a sign that we don't have enough faith in our own. To get agitated and angry when opposed shows a certain insecurity. If we really believe what we believe, we will not be shaken when someone challenges it.

Gandhi was an excellent example of this. It is said that he was at his best when he was criticized; it made him even more respectful and compassionate, and made him reach deeper into himself to find new ways of answering. I try to practice that in all kinds of little ways. Every day, for example, I look at a very influential newspaper whose editorial viewpoint contradicts everything I stand for. And I enjoy it: the writing is often excellent, and the differences in perspective help me to understand opinions I would otherwise never hear. I can give full attention to opposite opinions, and learn from them, because my faith in spiritual values is unshakable.

The reason for this, of course, is that these are not just my values. They are timeless, and my faith in them comes from many centuries of experience. If somebody challenges what I say about heaven being within, I don't get upset. It is Jesus who said it, and he is quite capable of defending his words himself.

Many years ago, I had a friend from Chicago who came to hear my talks in Berkeley every week. When he was about to return to Chicago he came up to say good-bye. "I've really enjoyed your talks," he told me. "And I like your sense of humor. But you know, I still don't believe a word of what you say."

I laughed and wished him well. Nobody likes to hear about self-will.

About twelve years later that fellow showed up again, looking much more than twelve years older. There were tears in his eyes when he came up to me and said, "Every word you say is true."

I comforted him by saying, "They are not really my words. They are the words of the great spiritual teachers in all religions, who have verified them over and over in their own lives. It takes most of us a certain amount of suffering to learn that they are true."

Even those who profess no religion can come to these same conclusions. Here is an outburst from one of my favorites in my college days, George Bernard Shaw:

> This is the true joy in life, the being used for a purpose recognized by yourself as a mighty one; the being thoroughly worn out before you are thrown on the scrap heap; the being a force of nature instead of a feverish selfish little clod of ailments and grievances complaining that the world will not devote itself to making you happy.

But security means much, much more than confidence in one's views. It pays richly in personal relationships. People with little self-will are so tremendously secure that they do not rely on other people to satisfy their needs. They will never try to manipulate you, and they are free to be loyal always. They will stand by you through thick and thin; you know you can count on them, no matter what the situation.

This kind of confidence is the very basis of love. Without this foundation, every relationship is apt to wane. You may honestly believe that this particular friendship is forever; this is what you have always been looking for. But whatever you want to believe, the nature of the mind is to change, and the more self-willed your mind is, the more likely it is to change its tune when things do not work out just right. Somebody once came to my talk on meditation and told me afterward, "This is what I have been looking for all my life!" She must have gone home and thought about it, because I am still looking for *her*.

★

All of us have tasted the freedom and happiness that self-forgetfulness brings, although we may not have known it at the time. In watching a good game of tennis or becoming engrossed in a novel, for example, the satisfaction comes not so much from what we are watching or reading as from the act of absorption itself. For that brief span, our burden of personal thoughts, worries, and conflicts is forgotten: and then we find relief, for what lies beneath that burden is the still, clear state of awareness we call joy. The scientist doing concentrated research, the artist absorbed in creative work, is happy because she has forgotten herself in what she is doing. Einstein had this genius for absorption in surprising measure.

But nowhere will you find personalities so joyous, so unabashedly lighthearted, as with those who have lost themselves in love for all. That is the universal appeal of Saint Francis of Assisi, the perfect image of his Master. In our own time, many millions have glimpsed this kind of joy in the film footage of Mother Teresa. To look into the eyes of men and women like these is to *see* what joy means.

After centuries of civilization, you would think we would have discovered that there is only one way to be completely happy, and that is to forget ourselves in working for others. It's a perplexing paradox: so long as we try to make ourselves happy, life places obstacles in our path. But the moment we turn away from ourselves to make others happy, our troubles melt away. Then we don't have to go looking for joy; joy comes looking for us.

In any age you will find a few men and women who have this marvelous gift of self-forgetfulness. In our own century there is the luminous figure of Gandhi, whom I met and walked with as a college student when I visited his ashram at Sevagram. The experience had a tremendous impact on my life. Gandhi had spent the day in meetings with political leaders who came to him for guidance in matters that affected the lives of four hundred million people; I expected to see him emerge in the evening tired and burdened. I could scarcely believe my eyes when the door swung open and Gandhi burst through, radiant and vital, joking as if he had been relaxing all day. When the time came for his evening walk, most of us had to run to keep up with this diminutive, frail-looking giant who carried the burdens of a continent with effortless grace.

It was in the evening prayer meeting that I began to understand his secret. Gandhi was seated in his usual place beneath a tree, and as the tropical sun disappeared, men and women around him took turns reciting prayers or singing hymns from different religious faiths. The atmosphere was charged. Although Gandhi neither spoke nor moved, I could not take my eyes off him as his secretary, Mahadev Desai, began to recite his favorite verses from the Bhagavad Gita, which begin:

> He lives in wisdom
> Who sees himself in all and all in him,

Whose love for the Lord of Love has consumed
Every selfish desire and sense craving
Tormenting the heart. . . .

Gandhi's eyes closed in meditation, and he slipped into such deep absorption that he scarcely seemed to breathe. Suddenly I understood what I was seeing: he had forgotten himself completely in those words, which embodied the ideals of his life, and in that absorption all the burdens a person might carry in such work were lifted from his shoulders as if by the Lord himself. It was a complete renewal.

Gandhi did not try to conceal his secret. "I am trying to reduce myself to zero," he said again and again; and in making himself zero, his love expanded to embrace the world. "My life is an indivisible whole, and all my activities run into one another; and they all have their rise in my insatiable love of mankind."

Remember Tauler's words: when we get ourselves out of the way, "God *must* fill up the void" – and the less there is of ourselves, the more he can pour in. For most of us, the idea of making ourselves zero sounds unattractive until we actually see someone like Gandhi. Then it is abundantly clear that this is not lack of personality but its fulfillment in joy.

These are secrets which the practice of meditation can slowly reveal to us. As we penetrate the layers of self-willed conditioning in our own consciousness and begin to see the divinity within, we see beneath these layers in everybody else as well. Then we realize that our own deepest needs – for love, harmony, meaning, peace of mind – are their needs too. The welfare of family and community and planet becomes more important to us than our own, for in it our own welfare is included. All this leaves very little time to think about ourselves, and that is the secret of happiness.

It is from this kind of giving that joy comes: not from having a lot of desires that must be satisfied, but from reducing personal desires to free time and energy for helping those around us. If I may illustrate with my own small example, I have enjoyed all the satisfactions that a person in India could have. I come from an ancient and very loving family and benefited from a good education, which gave me the best in both Indian and Western culture. As a university professor, sharing with young people my love of literature, and as a writer and public speaker, I achieved success in the fields I loved most. By Indian standards, I had everything one could desire. So I speak with an authentic voice when I say that today, when my personal desires are zero, the joy and love that I enjoy are, to quote the Upanishads, a million times what they were then. Every day my life is a million times richer.

All of us, when we hear talk like this, whisper in a quiet corner of our hearts, "Give up *all* personal desires? Can't I keep one or two of my favorites and settle for just five hundred times more joy?" This is a reasonable question. It takes many years of meditation to see that no matter how pleasant it may seem to indulge ourselves, every selfish craving is a thirst that cannot be quenched, a hunger that gnaws relentlessly at our peace of mind.

Once we grasp this deep in consciousness, there surges in our heart an even more powerful force: the desire to go against all selfish desires, to be free from cravings once and for all. Every step we take toward this goal brings such a sense of relief that today, one of my few personal prayers is to ask my Lord, "Never let me fall into the snare of selfish desires again!" I want every one of my desires to be for the welfare of all: that is what gives my life joy and meaning and fills my heart with love.

In the end, the goal of all spiritual seeking is to live in this state of self-forgetfulness permanently. This continuous awareness of God is to be achieved not after death, but here and now; that is what brings heaven on earth.

The Buddha uses the much-misunderstood word *nirvana* to describe this simple miracle. *Nir* means "out"; *vana*, "to blow": attaining nirvana means blowing out the burning flame of self-will, making ourselves poor in selfhood so as to be rich in God. But this is not just an idea from the mysterious East. Here is Saint Teresa of Avila on that state:

> While the mind is separated from itself, and while it is borne away into the secret place of the divine mystery and is surrounded on all sides by the fire of divine love, it is inwardly penetrated and inflamed by this fire, and utterly puts off itself and puts on a divine love. Thus conformed to the beauty it has beheld, it passes utterly into that other glory.

And here is Louis de Blois, a Benedictine monk who lived in sixteenth-century France:

> When through love the soul goes beyond all working of the intellect and all images in the mind, and is rapt above itself, utterly leaving itself, it flows into God: then is God its peace and fullness. It loses itself in the infinite solitude and darkness of the Godhead; but so to lose itself is rather to find itself. The soul is, as it were, all God-colored, because its essence is bathed in the essence of God.

The Lord's Prayer says plainly, "Thy will be done." But before his will can be done, our will – self-will – has to go. William Law put it precisely: "To sum up all in a word: nothing hath separated us from God but our own will, or rather our own will is our separation from God."

Here, again, we must remember that words like *Lord* and *God* do not refer to some higher being in another galaxy. We are talking about a barrier that separates us from our own deepest self, the very source and ground of what makes us human and gives meaning to our lives. Therefore, Eckhart says, "the soul is blessed perfectly when it follows the revelation of God back to the source from whence it came, their common origin, letting go of its own things and cleaving to his, so that the soul is blessed by God's things and not its own."

The more self-will we have, the more difficult it must be to trace consciousness back to its source. What would you think of trying to climb Mount Everest with a trunk full of memorabilia strapped to your back? Self-will weighs us down not a bit less, and the "ascent of Mount Carmel," as John of the Cross called it, begins with lightening the load.

None of us need feel disheartened when we begin to see that our self-will is grossly inflated. That is the human condition, and it gives no reason to give up and accommodate ourselves to living at the spiritual equivalent of sea level. All of us can learn to reduce this excess baggage and climb.

Self-will, in other words, is not something we have to learn to live with. It can be reduced to a bare minimum, even eliminated entirely, and every step of this reduction allows the radiance of personality to shine a little brighter.

Let me suggest three effective ways in which this can be done.

1. Meditation

The purpose of meditating on an inspirational passage such as the Beatitudes or the Prayer of Saint Francis is to empty the mind gradually of all thoughts other than the words of the passage. As Gandhi said, we are emptying the mind little by little, like a man emptying the sea with a cup. Thomas Merton quotes Dom Gueranger's beautiful description of this purpose:

> The words of God, of the saints, as we repeat them over and over again and enter more and more deeply into

their meaning, have a supreme grace to deliver the soul sweetly from preoccupation with itself in order to charm it and introduce it into the very mystery of God and of His Christ.

This process takes years, perhaps a lifetime. But benefits accrue from the very beginning. As preoccupation with ourselves diminishes, security builds. We find we have greater patience – and not just with others, but with ourselves as well. Things that used to cause stress and agitation no longer ruffle us, and people we used to find difficult start to show a brighter side. For all these reasons, and others too, our personal relationships blossom; and that, for many of us, is the richest dividend of all.

Gradually the day will come when you sit down for meditation and find your attention growing completely absorbed in the words of the inspirational passage. You will not hear the cars on the road nearby, or the planes flying overhead; you will not be aware of the chair you are sitting on. You will not even be aware of your body – and when you forget your body, you no longer live in the physical world.

When concentration is complete like this, not only space but time ceases to exist. You cannot think about the past or the future; every ray of attention is focused on the present moment. When there is no past, then no ghosts from the past – in particular, no anger or resentment – can come to make your life miserable. And when there is no future, there can be no anxiety or fear. In the mystics' language, you are delivered from the burden of time into the eternal Now.

It is not that you forget what happened yesterday when you lose the bond with the past; you just don't think about yesterday. And once your mind has learned not to think about yesterday, most internal conflicts evaporate.

It is as simple as that, because thinking about them is what makes them so real and oppressive. When meditation becomes so profound that the past falls away, old conflicts and the residue of emotional entanglements will fall away too. This "unburdening of memory," as John of the Cross calls it, brings an immense relief from the burden of past mistakes.

Similarly, it is heaven to be free of worry about tomorrow. I have many responsibilities, but I don't worry about them. I plan, I work hard, but I don't get anxious about results. When you develop this marvelous capacity to hold attention steady on the present, like the flame of a candle in a windless place, most anxieties evaporate. There is no reason to worry about what tomorrow may bring. If you live today completely in love – hating no one, hurting no one, serving all – then tomorrow *has* to be good, whatever comes.

2. *Slowing Down*

Living completely in the present, of course, is possible only with a quiet mind. The reason it is important to go through the words of a meditation passage *slowly* is to put a brake on the restless rush of the mind.

The faster thoughts go, the less control we have over them; that is what leaves decisions in the hands of dubious drivers like self-will. All negative thoughts are fast. Fear, resentment, greed, and jealousy rush through the mind at a hundred miles an hour. At such speeds we cannot turn, cannot stop, cannot keep from crashing into people. In fact, at speeds like this we are not really driving at all. We are hostages, trussed up in the trunk, and self-will is at the wheel.

If only I could show you what I see going on in the mind when someone gets angry! It is like watching thoughts whirling around in one of those clothes dryers at the laundromat, tumbling faster and faster. When the mind gets going like this, we have no more self-control or sensitivity to others than Conan the Barbarian.

Fast thinking has implications for the body too. People whose thoughts spin faster and faster become victims of the speed habit of their minds. Eventually any little thing can upset them – trifles and pinpricks that they should laugh about, if they notice them at all. This kind of turmoil takes a heavy toll on health, and evidence suggests that emotional instability may leave the body more vulnerable to illness and reduce its capacity for healing. Uncontrollable anger, for example, seems to be associated with hypertension and heart disease and is a component in severe breathing problems. Mind and body are not separate; they are aspects of one organism, and problems in the mind, when they become chronic, cannot help but affect the body too.

Even good health, then, calls for slowing down – and not just in meditation. We have to learn to keep the mind from racing during the day, and that means slowing down the whole frantic pace of modern life. There is an intimate connection between a hectic life-style and a hectic mind. Get up early, have your meditation without hurrying, talk to your children at breakfast, be kind to those around you. Even if the coffee isn't quite perked, what does it matter? Harmony is more important. And get to work early enough to chat with your colleagues; take a little time to get to know them better. You will find all this extremely useful in reducing self-will. When you are always in a rush, you cannot handle self-will because you cannot even see others' needs. You don't have time to be thoughtful or kind.

When meditation deepens, thoughts begin to slow down naturally. Then the temperature of self-will begins to drop. I wish I had a thermometer that could measure this. If genetic engineers can make biochemical markers in tobacco plants glow in the dark, why can't we have a gauge to show when self-will is heating up? As a matter of fact, with a little detached observation, it is not hard to see this happening in someone else. There are all kinds of signs, though some vary from person to person, and one sure pattern is that all the machinery of body and mind speeds up, from heart rate to speech. The trick is to be detached enough to see this happening in ourselves – and then be able to take steps promptly to correct it.

Here the mantram offers immediate, effective first aid. When you find self-will rising – when you find yourself getting angry or afraid, or some strong desire is about to get out of control, or you feel you have to get your way or you will explode – start repeating your mantram, or Holy Name, in your mind and, if possible, head for the door for a good, fast walk around the block. (Walking is one thing it's good to do fast, particularly a mantram walk at emergency time.)

Hold on to your mantram as if your life depended on it – in some respects it really might. You will find that there is a close connection between the rhythm of the mantram, the rhythm of your footsteps, the rhythm of your breathing, and the rhythm of your mind. Walk briskly, and keep going for at least a good two or three turns around the block. Quickly you will find these rhythms blending, steadying your breathing rate and slowing down the furious pace of your thoughts. By the time you get back your mind will be clearer, and a good deal of your agitation will have quieted down – simply by slowing down the mind.

I have seen people do this in the midst of an impossible situation and come back calmer in just fifteen minutes – forgiving instead of angry, kind and creative instead of frustrated and hostile. That is the power of the mantram, and the effect on other people involved has to be seen to be believed.

3. Putting Others First

A third way to dissolve the strata of self-centered conditioning is by learning to think of other people's needs before our own. This is perhaps the most important, the most difficult, and the most rewarding challenge on the spiritual path. Tender, truly loving relationships are the essence of serving the Lord in all.

The longer you go on meditating, the more you will see that whenever there is a problem in personal relationships, the cause is not really differences of opinion or life-style; it is self-will. A large ego – mammoth self-will – is like one of those mobile homes you sometimes see under tow on the freeway, with red flags sticking out on both sides. I try to move into the lane farthest away from them, even before I get close enough to see the sign that warns, "Wide Load." They can suddenly invade your space, drifting into your lane. Unfortunately, some people are like that too. With so much emphasis on being aggressive and competitive, on "doing your own thing" and "looking out for number one," millions of people have developed such rampant self-will that they too ought to carry little red flags in their belts, so that others can give them plenty of room to maneuver.

On the other hand, there are a few rare people who will give you their lane if necessary and say, "We'll pull over; you go ahead." Jesus says that these are the people who live in heaven. They don't just drive off onto the shoulder and give up the road; they have a destination too, and it is important for them to get there. But they know how to yield gracefully, how to look far ahead and undo a dangerous situation when they see an accident coming. Such people not only are safe drivers, they make the road safer for the rest of us as well.

If just one person in the family does this, a home becomes heaven. Even an office can become heaven! Putting others first is an infectious example that affects everybody around. In Berkeley in the sixties, an institution sprang up called the Free University. All of us maintain a free university of our own, where we teach by what we are. Especially where children are concerned, the home is a seven-day-a-week school of education for living.

But putting others first does not mean telling them yes all the time. Love often shows itself in the inward toughness that is required to say no to an attitude or desire that we think will bring harm. Parents have to do this often, for children who grow up without hearing no from their parents will be terribly brittle when they have to take no from life itself – and, worse, they will have a hard time saying no to themselves.

But loving opposition, whether to children or to adults you live or work with, has to be done tenderly and without any anger or condescension. Otherwise you are likely only to be adding more self-will to the flames. This is a difficult art. Go slowly, and remember that it is always better not to act in the heat of the moment. Whenever time allows, instead of responding immediately to an unwise demand, take a mantram walk first, meditate, and then speak when you can do so with kindness and patience. Remember, too, that the very best way to change someone is to begin with your own example.

These are skills that everyone needs in order to love, and most of us have not learned them. Relationships break down easily today not because people are bad but because they are illiterate in love. Knowing how to read and write and manage a computer does not educate us for lasting relationships. To be literate in love, we have to learn to reduce self-will.

Today, after many, many years of experience, I can look at a romantic relationship and make a fairly accurate guess as to whether it will last. I don't even have to observe the couple during a crisis; their behavior in little everyday incidents tells me a great deal. All I have to do is ask myself, "Is each person ready to put the other first?" If the answer is yes, that relationship is likely to grow deeper and more rewarding with the passage of time, whatever problems may come. But if the answer is no, that relationship may not be able to withstand even a little of the testing that life is bound to bring. Though I may not be able to predict the specific incident, sooner or later, self-will may rebel when things don't go its way.

I have heard the most cultured people, in the most affectionate of relationships, saying hurtful things, simply because they have not learned to train the mind never to indulge in any kind of harm. That is the purpose of meditation. "When a man's ways please the Lord," the Bible says, "He maketh even his enemies to be at peace with him." That is a beautiful insight into the trained mind. Today everything I do is to please the Lord, so my life is very simple. It is not that I don't face complicated problems; every day life brings increasing challenges, but I have learned to face them without inner turmoil. All I do is ask what would please my Lord. I am no longer interested in pleasing myself or in pleasing anybody else in particular; I want only to please God.

Putting others first is an area in which the mind can often play tricks on us. Interestingly enough, often when we think we are thinking of others, putting their needs first, we are really just trying to please – which means we are really thinking about ourselves. You can see how slippery self-will can be.

"Nothing burns in hell but self-will." What penetrating words! An outburst of self-will may seem justified at the time, but for those who are sensitive, a stab of remorse follows all too soon. This is a good sign. It is much better to be sensitive, suffer from our mistakes, and learn not to repeat them than to go through life leaving a trail of broken relationships and wondering why we hurt inside.

This way of learning is terribly painful, but almost all of us should expect it. I, for one, did not manage to avoid it. My mother must have been born kind; in seventy years I don't remember her uttering a hurtful word to anyone. But I was like everyone else. As children do, I sometimes said hurtful things that I was ashamed of afterward, and when I did it would torment me. I would toss and turn throughout the night, and the next morning I would go straight to my cousin or whoever it was and say, "I hope what I said yesterday didn't hurt you." To make it worse, he would look at me blankly and ask, "What was it?"

I used to complain to my grandmother, "This isn't fair! *He* is the one who should feel hurt, and he doesn't even remember it. Why should I be the one who can't sleep?"

"That is the makings of what is in store for you," she would say mysteriously. "That is the way you learn." I didn't understand, and I could never get her to explain.

But she was right: my motivation grew. If somebody said something rude to me, I learned to hold back a rude response and think, "Oh, no. I don't want to lie awake at night!" That is how it began. Today that reversal of conditioning has gone so far that if someone says or does something unkind to me, I feel sorry for that person, not for myself.

Self-will, the mystics say, will always cause us pain. The least we can do is learn from it. When you make a mistake and cannot sleep at night because of it, use the power of your pain to drive your mantram deep into your consciousness, where it can heal the wound and help bring the desire not to act on self-will again. The purpose of suffering is for us to learn one of life's most important lessons: as Jesus patiently points out again and again, it is much better to suffer and learn than to cause suffering to those around us. That is why you will never hear a good spiritual teacher asking anybody, "Are you having fun?" The real question is, Are you growing? If you are, well and good, even if it hurts. If we could grow up by having fun, I would be all for it. Unfortunately, however, a diet of fun often stunts human growth.

Lessons like these are learned partly at night, when the past may not let us rest, and that is where the mantram is invaluable. Scientists are doing significant research in the realm of sleep, but I don't think the modern world yet knows as much about sleep as these lovers of God. Saint Francis said that particularly at night, he felt the pain of Christ in his own body – the suffering of Him who bore in himself the sorrows of all the world. That is how far sensitivity can go. Few of us aspire to those rare heights, but all of us suffer in our sleep more than we know, when hurtful things we have done and said follow us into deeper consciousness. Recently I came across a haunting passage from the Greek tragedian Aeschylus:

> . . . And even in our sleep pain that cannot forget falls drop by drop upon the heart, and in our own despair, against our will, comes wisdom to us by the awful grace of God.

This happens much more often than we are aware of, particularly when we become more sensitive to our own self-will as meditation deepens. Sleep then becomes an important part of spiritual growth.

Here a little preparation can go a long, long way. When you are ready for bed, there are a few simple things you can do to make your night better.

First, have your meditation again in the evening for half an hour. As Gandhi said, we should make prayer the key of our morning and the bolt of our evening.

Then do a little spiritual reading, even if only for fifteen minutes. Choose something that is completely positive and inspiring, either a passage from the scriptures or the direct words of a great mystic who has realized God. There is great poetry in the mystics, delicious humor, profound insight, words with life and power of their own to seal your day with a lofty image of what the human being can become.

Then, after you put your book aside and tuck yourself in, close your eyes and start repeating your mantram until you fall asleep in it.

This is not as easy as it may sound. Other thoughts will try to push the mantram away. But through sheer persistence you can achieve a minor miracle. Between the last waking moment and the first sleeping moment, there is an arrow's entry into deepest consciousness. If you can send your mantram in through that narrow gate, it will go on repeating itself throughout the night, healing old wounds and restoring your soul for the next day. Those who have learned to do this, in Brother Lawrence's phrase, go forward even in their sleep.

Today, after many years of practice, my mantram stands at the entrance to my mind throughout the night. If negative thoughts come, it just says, "Sorry, you need a pass." Don't bouncers work as long as the bar is open? The mantram too is quite happy to work all night, and when you fall asleep in it, the name of the Lord will run through your mind until you wake up, healing body and mind with its quiet harmony.

This is a harsh world we live in. People have grown used to using rough, unkind language and to doing harmful things. If you can remember not to retaliate in words and actions, eventually you will find it impossible even to think hurtful thoughts. Then your self-will is nearly zero, and instead of causing others pain, your very presence will help and heal. This is the extraordinary light that mysticism throws on the human mind: as self-will is reduced, what shines forth is love. You don't have to borrow it from the saints and stuff it into your consciousness. It is there in all of us, if only we are willing to get ourselves out of the way.

Simplicity

*Blessed are the meek, for they shall inherit
the earth.*

ON JANUARY 2, 1989, *Time* magazine skipped its
customary cover feature on the Man or Woman of the
Year. Instead, the cover illustration showed the Planet of
the Year: an "Endangered Earth" trussed up in string, the
subject of stories on threats to its life and welfare that had
dominated the news in the previous twelve months.

This break in tradition was not prompted by any one
particular event: not the nuclear accident at Chernobyl,
which may take its toll for generations, or even the ongo-
ing loss of our tropical forests, an ecological folly which
might wipe out half of the species of life on earth and turn
present croplands to deserts. What prompted *Time*'s
choice was not so much catastrophes like these as the in-
numerable accidents and incidents which keep coming to
remind us that the "acceptable risks" of modern civilization may add up to an uninhabitable world.

One such accident, still vivid in my memory, was the
industrial fire in Switzerland in 1986 which spilled some

thirty tons of deadly chemicals into the Rhine. This beautiful river, famed in song and legend, was polluted with poisons whose cumulative effects are unknown. Millions of fish were killed, and decades will pass before we know what damage has been done to the microorganisms which form the basis of the river's ecosystem. In West Germany alone, more than forty thousand villages lost their supply of drinking water.

I have seen the effects of some of these disasters with my own eyes. Not long ago, for example, some of the most beautiful beaches of northern California were engulfed in a huge oil slick, washed northward from an exploded tanker that sank outside the Golden Gate. On the islands and coastlands, some of which are wildlife refuges, one could see seabirds trapped in oozing slime. Hundreds of volunteers turned out to rescue these graceful creatures – seagulls, godwits, sandpipers, and the like – carefully wiping the brownish-gray scum off their bodies; for if its wings are seriously encumbered, a seabird dies.

Aside from the ecological tragedy, the confusion visible in these birds haunted me for a long time. How close their plight is to that of the human being! As Thomas a Kempis reminds us, the soul requires two wings to soar above the pull of worldly things. One is purity, which enables us to keep our eyes on the divinity in every human being. The other is simplicity: and not merely in our life-style, John of the Cross would say, but simplicity in our desires; for having many desires, often at cross purposes, is what creates complication and confusion in our lives.

Neither of these qualities, Thomas implies, is enough in itself to lift us up. If either is weak, we will flounder on the beach like one of those poor tarred birds. But together, when they are strong, purity and simplicity enable the soul to soar aloft.

In the name of simplification today we are asked to take

the most remarkable steps: to buy food processors and microwave ovens, open charge accounts, install a telephone in every room, pay a travel agent to plan our next vacation down to the last waiter's tip. It is exhilarating to be reminded here that the real meaning of simplicity is singling out what is worth living for, and then shaping our lives around what matters and letting go of everything else.

Thoreau tells us in clear, haunting words, "I went to the woods because I wished to live deliberately, to front only the essential facts of life, and see if I could not learn what it had to teach, and not, when I came to die, discover that I had not lived." What *are* the essentials of life? What must we learn if we really mean to live?

"The earth is the Lord's," says the psalmist, "and the fullness thereof; the world, and they that dwell therein." Familiar words – perhaps too familiar. Do we hear them question the basis of our lives? Seas, mountains, forests, air, other people and other creatures: all these belong not to us, but to the Lord. You and I are just tenants here, with rights of tenancy, no doubt, but with responsibilities too. Our divine landlord expects us to look after our home, this green earth. And we are not doing a very good job.

One of the most impressive things about the Rhine pharmaceutical plant accident was its impact. The story attracted press attention around the world, but by the next week, except in the countries immediately affected, it was all but forgotten. Only a few concerned voices were heard to plead that these are not just noteworthy incidents, but clues to a larger pattern. Industrial technology is like a drug. Drugs cause a cluster of actions in the body, some of them intended and others incidental to the purpose, but it is only in the mind that the "side effects" can be separated from the effects that we desire. Ecological effects too are as much a part of industrial production as the plastics and chemical creations that justify it in our eyes. The more we depend on those products, the greater the impact on the environment has to be – and soon, the litany of the news reminds us, we had better assess the total cost.

"Well," we ask, "if we don't like the cost, what are we supposed to learn from ruined rivers and air that's not fit to breathe? What is the planet trying to tell us?" The answer is "Simplify your lives." Industrial technology has a welcome place in helping to make life safer and more comfortable, but when we let it get out of control it becomes the world's greatest enemy. Technology is not an end in itself. It is a means to an end, and that end is human health, happiness, and welfare. When it begins to produce the opposite results, it is time to decide how much we really need. Technology should be not our master but our servant.

A simple life does not mean a life of poverty. There is plenty of room for material comfort and personal satisfaction while living lightly on the planet, making a contribution to life instead of threatening it. Simple living, to me, is the art of using minimum means to attain maximum results – just the opposite of what happens when we get caught up in the obsessions of a consumer society. Later in this chapter I will suggest some ways to simplify while living life at its richest.

To live simply is to live gently, keeping in mind always the needs of the planet, other creatures, and the generations to come. In doing this we lose nothing, because the interests of the whole naturally include our own.

"Blessed are the meek, for they shall inherit the earth." The danger facing our planet lends new meaning to Jesus' words. Most of us are properly suspicious when someone tells us to be "meek" or "humble"; it sounds unctuous and just the opposite of strong. Charles Dickens has a curious character called Uriah Heep who is always proclaiming

how "'umble" he is. His job is 'umble, his home is 'umble, his character is 'umble. All he really is, unfortunately, is 'ypocritical. No one wants to be like Uriah Heep.

Yet the meekness that Jesus suggests is a most attractive quality. Like "poor in spirit," it means the absence of self-will, the opposite of the kind of personality that asserts its dominance over everything and everyone around. It is not the arrogant that shall inherit the earth, but those who are gentle with its resources and its creatures. In claiming nothing for themselves, they have everything, for everything is theirs to enjoy as part of the whole.

Saint John of the Cross tells us in Zen-like terms:

> In order to arrive at having pleasure in everything,
> Desire to have pleasure in nothing.
> In order to arrive at possessing everything,
> Desire to possess nothing.
> In order to arrive at being everything,
> Desire to be nothing. . . .

"To enjoy everything, desire to get joy from nothing." If it sounds unattractive, that is only because we don't understand. The key is our desires: are they self-directed, or are they for all? Don't ask life to please you, John is telling us; ask how you can give. Then you are free to enjoy in good times and bad, in ups and downs, whatever life brings. Desire nothing just for yourself; then the whole world is yours. It multiplies joy a millionfold, and no one has proclaimed the joy of it more gloriously than the English mystic Thomas Traherne:

> You never enjoy the world aright, till you see how a
> sand exhibiteth the power and wisdom of God . . . till
> every morning you awake in Heaven; see yourself in
> your Father's Palace; and look upon the skies, the earth,
> and the air as Celestial Joys. . . . You never enjoy the
> world aright, till the Sea itself floweth in your veins, till
> you are clothed with the heavens, and crowned with the
> stars: and perceive yourself to be the sole heir of the

whole world, and more than so, because men are in it who are every one sole heirs as well as you. . . . Till your spirit filleth the whole world, and the stars are your jewels; . . . till you love men so as to desire their happiness, with a thirst equal to the zeal of your own; till you delight in God for being good to all: you never enjoy the world.

Traherne and Saint John give us a glimpse of the towering strength and self-control that gentleness and humility require. The stamp of the mystic, if I may put it paradoxically, is a proud humility. Francis of Assisi erased every trace of ego from his personality; yet no one was ever more personal, and Francis carried himself through life with the proud assurance that, in the words of Saint Paul, "not I, but Christ liveth in me."

Mahatma Gandhi had the same combination of humility and unshakable self-assurance. When he was asked if he were free from ambition, he replied, "Oh, no! I am the most ambitious man in the world. I want to make myself zero." I used to remind myself of this in the early days of my meditation, when many relatives and friends said, "You have such promise; why do you want to throw all this away? Don't you have any ambition?" I wanted to tell them that my ambition was only beginning. Previously I had wanted only to be a good teacher and a great writer, perhaps win the Nobel Prize in literature; now I wanted to make myself zero like Gandhi.

The source of this "proud humility" is the awareness of the divine spark within our heart. With that at our center, what can we not do? George Bernard Shaw wrote: "We need men who can dream of things that never were, and ask why not." That is the spirit of this "meekness" that Jesus extols. In this country of ambitious people, I may be the most ambitious of all, for I believe that you and I, in our own lifetime, can make our streets safe and bring harmony to our homes, simplicity to our lives, and depth to our personal relationships. We can clean up the environment for our children and grandchildren. And I won't be content with just a nuclear freeze; I want to banish war itself. So if people tell you that meditation stifles motivation, you can tell them that this is what motivating forces like ambition are really for: to stir us to action on behalf of all.

It is when these instincts are harnessed for the welfare of the whole that we get the fullest reward life can give. Ambition for oneself only makes a person narrower. It is when our desires reach out to embrace all of life that life fulfills them – and much more generously than we could ever anticipate. "God is ready to give great things," says Eckhart, "when we are ready, for righteousness' sake, to give up everything."

This message is repeated again and again in the teachings of the great religions: it is when we live to serve the Lord in all that we inherit our full legacy of joy. When Gandhi was challenged to sum up the secret of his life in three words, he replied with a quote from an Indian scripture, the Isha Upanishad: "Renounce and enjoy!" These lines, he said, contain all the wisdom we need to steer a safe course through the crises of our industrial age:

> The Lord is enshrined in the hearts of all.
> The Lord is the supreme reality.
> Rejoice in him through renunciation.
> Covet nothing. All belongs to the Lord.
> Thus working may you live a hundred years.
> Thus alone will you work in real freedom.

★

"The earth is the Lord's, and the fullness thereof." If we take these words as more than just poetry, they mean that you and I are just trustees. The resources of our planet have been entrusted to every one of us together, and like any good bank trustee, we are expected not to squander them but to invest them wisely for our beneficiaries: the rest of life, especially the generations to come.

This view has far-reaching consequences. The trust includes not simply the lives and resources of the planet, but inner resources too. The fact that nothing on earth belongs to us personally has some very practical implications, all of which come down to a simpler life: simpler in its externals, and so gentler on the earth; but simpler too in our inner lives, where desires are fewer but immeasurably richer and more productive.

To begin with, when you regard your life as a trust, you realize that the first resource you have to take care of is your own body.

This can be startling. Even your body is not really your own. It belongs to life, and it is your responsibility to take care of it. You cannot afford to do anything that injures your body, because the body is the instrument you need for selfless action. That is the fine print of the trust agreement: when we smoke, when we overeat, when we don't get enough exercise, we are violating the terms of the trust. If you want to live life at its fullest, you will want to do everything possible to keep your body in vibrant health in order to give back to life a little of what it has given you.

This approach has helped thousands of people I know to give up harmful habits such as smoking and drinking, without my ever preaching at them or belittling them. I keep my eye on that core of goodness. Life is crying for the contribution of every one of us, and it stirs people to learn that most of us have no idea of the capacities we have hidden inside, or what tremendous energy can be released when we free ourselves from habits that drain our energy and tie our hands. When we begin to simplify our lives, ways of giving back to life appear without our ever having to ask.

In everything, simplicity is the key to trusteeship. A simple life conserves not just our personal resources but the earth's.

A good place to begin simplifying is with this "frenzy of consumerism," to use Pope John Paul II's apt phrase – this endless cycle of buying and producing beyond any reasonable need. Everywhere I see shopping malls cropping up like alien mushrooms. I can appreciate the convenience of a pleasant, sheltered place with a few good shops selling useful things, but how many do we really need? When I go to a mall I don't often see people come to get the thing they need and then go home. Many come just to pass the time, looking for something to spend money on.

It is not only money that is thrown away in "recreational shopping"; this aimless activity is such a tragic waste of time and attention. When shoppers go home, they leave part of their capacity to love behind in the shopping mall. Even if they don't spend money, they spend their energy. Only when this fever of buying and accumulating things quiets down can we begin to give that energy and attention to family and community, where they are desperately needed. If each of us can simplify in little ways, far-reaching changes are within our power.

Take gift giving, for example. Is it really necessary to celebrate every birthday, anniversary, promotion, and "holiday" established by a greeting card manufacturer with a gift that is often neither useful nor desired? Why not give a gift of ourselves – of our time, attention, thoughtfulness, affection? "The most sublime act," wrote William Blake, "is to set another before you." If you have grown estranged from someone, you can move a little closer; you can begin paying attention to those you have ignored. And beyond the circle of those we live and work with, there are a great many people who desperately need love and attention and no end of deserving causes that need help.

This is one of the hidden problems of consumerism: it wastes the time and drains the energy we need for personal relationships. I don't think most people realize how much vitality can trickle away in a visit to the shopping mall. It's not only buying; just gauge how you feel at the end of a day of window-shopping. In terms of the impact on your personal energy reserves, you have written a big energy check and handed it over just for the time spent, even if you never wrote a check for a purchase and took things home.

A good deal of vitality escapes through the eyes, especially when desire comes into play. One simple tactic of defensive shopping, then, is to keep close watch over what your eyes are doing. Don't waste time and energy letting your eyes wander and then find that your mind and your desires have ambled along after. Don't let yourself be taken in by advertising tactics designed to make you pick up carefully placed "impulse" items. Keep your mantram going, keep your attention on what you are there for, get it, pay for it, and leave. When you get home, not only your checking account but your energy level will be relatively intact, leaving you more to spend where it really counts.

But the worst threat from a consumer society is the toll it takes on the environment: in the burning of fossil fuels, in the release of toxic industrial wastes, and finally in the problems of how to get rid of the trash. I am not against buying things that are needed; my objection is that so many of the items produced for us to buy are neither necessary nor beneficial, and in environmental terms, all of us pay through the nose just to have them in the stores, whether we buy or not.

Now, none of these things is in the stores because manufacturers hate clean air. None of them is produced just to fill up chain store shelves. They are there because people buy them, and manufacturers will go on making more so long as we go on buying. To escape from this sad-go-round of pollution and waste is simple: we must each begin to weigh our desire for an item against what it costs the environment to produce it – and then start saying, "No, it's not worth it."

In other words – just as John of the Cross would have told us! – even cleaning up the environment leads to managing our desires. Simplifying life implies throwing out things and activities we do not need, but what goes furthest is cleaning out the mind. The mind is an immense garage stuffed with desires, and every one we manage to throw away means a pile of plastic that need never be produced because we have no compulsion to buy.

For many of my friends, the most persuasive side of this appeal is the benefit to the next generation. Each time you are about to make a purchase, ask yourself, "What will this cost our children in clean air and pure water?"

I read an excellent article by Carl Sagan and Ann Druyan which took this tack. On behalf of their young daughter and all the world's children, they appealed to the newly elected president of the United States: "Give Us Hope for the Future." "It is no longer enough to love, feed, shelter, clothe and educate a child – not when the future itself is in danger," they observed. "Being a conscientious parent today also means working to preserve and to protect the nation and the planet – now, before it's too late." They urged the president to recognize pollution as a crime against the future:

> We have been treating the environment as if there were
> no tomorrow – as if there will be no new generations to
> be sustained by the bounties of the Earth. But they, and
> we, must drink the water and breathe the air. . . .

I agree wholeheartedly with these concerns, but I do not expect government or industry to take the initiative in solving problems for us. My appeal is to the people. If we take these matters into our own hands, they can be dealt with without legislation or costly government intervention, which without our support might even make the situation worse. Problems like pollution do not appear out of nowhere. They develop through thousands of little, individual acts, and that is just how we can reverse them. In countless ways, each of us can begin to assume our trusteeship duties and take responsibility for the earth, air, and water.

Most of us, for example, do not give much thought to where our household trash goes after the truck pulls away. Yet what to do with the discards of industrial civilization already poses questions we cannot answer, and the problem is getting worse.

In 1988, *Time* magazine estimated that the amount of trash generated in this country had increased by eighty percent in the previous thirty years. The United States produces more trash per person than any other country – twice as much as Japan and West Germany – and we are running out of places to put it. About half the landfills in this country have already closed, and the Environmental Protection Agency predicts that one third of those remaining will be filled to capacity in five to ten years.

Now, I have always been proud of living in California, which produces such a rich variety of vegetables, fruits, nuts, and grains. When Indian friends ask me if I have become an American, I like to reply, "No, I have become a Californian." On this question, however, I have not. California evidently holds the world's record in the production of personal waste: about twenty-five pounds of trash per week from every man, woman, and child.

Some of this, apparently, could easily be recycled or composted: glass, paper and cardboard, newspapers, grass clippings from lawns. But recycling is only a partial solution. Much of the material we throw away is not recyclable or even biodegradable. It has to go somewhere, and as landfills close down, the temptation becomes stronger to ship it out on barges and dump it into the ocean. "Out of sight, out of mind." Perhaps, but not out of our lives. Trash dumped at sea is finding its way home. I have seen once-beautiful beaches looking like trash heaps – covered with junk, from "disposable" fast-food containers to dangerous medical waste – and beautiful marine animals such as seals and sea gulls choking on plastic bags and dying of chemical burns. I still remember a dying seal looking at me in mute appeal as if to say, "You people are supposed to protect us. You are the trustees of our world. Why aren't you doing your job?"

Some states and cities are passing strict antipollution laws, with stiff fines for offenders. Instead, why not generate less trash? If each of us produces twenty-five pounds of trash a week, why not begin by cutting it down to twenty? If you're meditating, you might aim at fifteen – or even ten. The connection with simplifying is plain: the less we bring home, the less we have to throw away; the less we buy, the less will be produced. Everybody can do this, and the spirit is contagious.

Similarly, there are lots of ways in which we can each help restore the purity of our air.

First of all, we can dramatically reduce both fossil fuel use and air pollution simply by cutting back on unnecessary driving. I have nothing against automobiles; it is our overuse of automobiles that is getting us into trouble, making the air more and more laden with smog, the freeways more and more congested. Cities counter by building more and wider roads, but this only adds to the problem by encouraging more cars. Southern California is a perfect example. In Los Angeles, which has grown on the promise of a lavish network of freeways, traffic is so thick that cars move at an average of thirty-three miles per hour – and by the year 2000 this rate is expected to drop to fifteen!

The San Francisco Bay Area is moving rapidly toward this kind of congestion, and planners talk of adding lanes to the highway. Meanwhile, every time I travel to the city I am struck by the spectacle of car after car after car with just one person inside. Common sense suggests a simple and elegant solution: why not travel two to a car? If everybody did it, we would have cut the traffic by half – and cut by half the tragic toll of traffic accidents, which, according to one commentator, can be compared to fighting the Vietnam War on our freeways every fourteen months.

If traveling two to a car can cut the problem in half, you can see how each member of a carpool counts. When I go to San Francisco, I usually take three or four friends along; I fill up the car. Carpooling is not only efficient and easy on the environment, it's good companionship. The extra fifteen minutes needed to drive a few miles to pick up a passenger, to wait a few moments if necessary, are not time wasted. I understand that each year the average American car pumps its own weight of carbon into the atmosphere. In those fifteen minutes you have kept one car off the road for one day; what could you have done in a quarter of an hour to make an impact like that? And if you use the time for repeating the mantram, you have added to your own spiritual growth as well.

Another alternative to cars – a favorite of mine – is trains. They can be made fast, efficient, safe, and clean, as we can see from what Japan has done. The railway system is beginning to expand here too, as more and more people discover how pleasant train travel can be. When I first came to this country, I traveled from New York to Kansas by train, then from Kansas to Minnesota and from there to California, and I enjoyed every hour. You can take your work along if you like; you can read, meditate, or play with your children.

Finally, I would like to put in a word for the simplest, safest, and surest mode of transportation ever: walking. Nothing beats walking for simplicity. You don't need any special equipment, only a good, comfortable pair of shoes; and you don't have to train for it or learn any special skills. The only novel suggestion I have about walking is to take the mantram along. Every morning after meditation, my wife and I start our day with a long, fast walk on the beach repeating our mantram. We have kept up this routine for the past twenty-five years, even in the sort of weather that makes one want to stay in bed. The earth is a joy in the quiet hours of early morning, and the mantram renews the mind; we come back full of energy for a long day of hard, selfless work.

Twenty-five years ago, even in California, we were looked upon as a trifle eccentric for doing this. Today, I am happy to report, brisk walking is recognized as one of the best forms of aerobic exercise you can get. Add the mantram and you get a near-perfect tonic for body, mind, and spirit at once. Just imagine: if you live within walking distance of your job, you can use your commute time for getting in shape and arrive at work refreshed and calm, even glowing. Little everyday errands can be opportunities for boosting your well-being while you help the environment. How often do we automatically hop into the car and drive a few blocks to mail a letter or pick up some groceries? In many cases, walking takes about the same amount of time.

In today's world we are getting hemmed in on all sides, and ironically, a lot of the hemming in comes from the automobile. I have read that the average person can now expect to spend about six months of his or her life just sitting behind the wheel waiting for red lights to change! Why not break free and walk or bicycle to the corner store? Your body will be strengthened and your nerves soothed, your senses will be sharpened and refreshed, and your heart will become more attuned to the rhythm of the seasons and the beauty of the Lord's creation.

A second way to restore the purity of the air is to protect trees, from your local juniper to the tropical rain forests that sustain life as we know it. These forests may be on the other side of the globe from most of us, but they affect our lives here and now – and our everyday behavior affects them too. Rain forests are disappearing at the rate of twenty-seven million acres per year – or, to bring the figures closer to home, we are losing an area of rain forest the size of a football field every second. Most of this destruction takes place just to raise cattle for beef, the majority of which winds up in American restaurants and delicatessens. Already two thirds of the rain forests in Central America have been lost to cattle pasture.

This kind of rampant deforestation is especially devastating because of what it does to the greenhouse effect – the overall warming of the globe, heightened by industrial pollution, which threatens to shift climate as drastically as the Ice Age. Slash-and-burn clearing methods release huge amounts of carbon into the air, increasing the global warming effect just the way a smokestack does. And, of course, such methods leave far fewer trees to take up the carbon dioxide and give back oxygen. In countries where deforestation has been allowed to continue, the results have been desertification, erosion, floods, and starvation.

Scientists are only beginning to discover the rich biological diversity hidden in these primordial forests; it is said they contain more than half of the known species of flora and fauna. Each year thousands of these species are destroyed forever, and we cannot even begin to guess at what effect these losses will have on the delicate balance of our ecosystem.

The picture is grim, but there is a bright side: everyone

can help directly, simply by switching to a vegetarian diet.

Vegetarianism is scarcely a deprivation today. With major health organizations like the American Cancer Society recommending that we eat less meat and more fresh fruits and vegetables, there are all kinds of good vegetarian cookbooks to show how delicious vegetarian cuisine can be.

Here is where the power of gentle persuasion can come into play. You can share your enthusiasm with your friends, and when you go out to eat, you can ask for vegetarian food. As more and more people do this, that is what restaurants will slowly begin to provide. When I first came to the Bay Area, people thought I had some ailment when I asked for vegetarian food. Today, with so many people asking, there are excellent vegetarian restaurants; some, in Berkeley and San Francisco, have a national reputation for excellence. That is what the demand of little people can do.

For me, the real joy of vegetarianism is knowing that my meals are not at the expense of any living creature. "All creatures love life," the Buddha says. "All creatures fear death. Therefore do not kill, or cause another to kill." Animals have as much joy in living as we have; if we have lost this perspective, it is simply because of our conditioning. Animals are not just animals to me: our scriptures call them "four-footed people." When I hear about the misery veal calves undergo, I feel almost as if they are crying out to me, "Please tell people that we love life too."

Besides not eating meat, everybody can help to reverse the greenhouse effect by simply planting a few trees. Experts say that urban tree planting can greatly reduce atmospheric carbon dioxide while helping keep the earth's surface cool. In urban areas, where there are few trees to offset the heating effect of cars and factories, temperatures are often as much as ten degrees higher than in the surrounding countryside. Planting trees can cut home energy bills as well. It has been shown, for example, that air-conditioning costs can be lowered by as much as half by planting a few shade trees on the southern and western sides of a house.

The American Forestry Association estimates that there are a hundred million spaces around American homes and communities where additional trees can be planted. We can each take part in this, and the children can join in too. Children love working side by side with adults in activities they know are meaningful. I learned this from my grandmother, who was the wisest child psychologist I have ever known; I enjoyed doing things with her much more than I ever liked playing with toys.

So please get together with your children and start planting trees. It is very inexpensive – just a few cents for a seedling – and the benefits are beyond calculation. Your children will enjoy the time you spend together, and fifteen years later they will remember the trees you planted together, which give them shade, save them energy, and fill their air with oxygen.

And why stop with trees? Gardening is another activity that anyone can share with family and friends. Growing your own food, as far as possible, and supporting growers who use organic methods, are simple and effective ways to reduce the problem of pesticide-tainted produce as well as the pollution of our water with runoff from agricultural chemicals. A small kitchen garden needn't take a great deal of space; even apartment dwellers can usually find room for a few containers. And in many areas, community gardens are springing up – a wonderful blend of good nutrition, recreation, and community spirit.

★

Simplifying your life, then, does not mean cutting back on anything of value. It means learning the delicate artistry of making your every action count, taking notice of the needs of the whole. You can think of it as a skill – and, as with any other skill, the more you practice it, the more opportunities you will find to put it to use, bringing your creativity and ingenuity into play.

This is one of the joys that come when you see your life as a trust. When your desires are focused on the welfare of the whole, all your faculties are magnified. Nothing is lost; on the contrary, your vitality and creativity increase, and so does the joy you feel at knowing you are leaving the world a little better, a little more hopeful, for those to come.

In this view, not even our time, talent, and resources are our personal property. They are precious resources that the Lord has given us in trust – meant to be spent freely, but for the benefit of all.

This throws fresh light on every aspect of life – our work, our relationships, and even the way we spend our leisure time. For example, I find it curious that people associate the idea of vacation with going somewhere else. For me, the very best vacation is to forget myself in working hard for a meaningful, selfless cause with people I know and love.

This is the kind of vacation I would like everybody to have: working to bring joy into the lives of others; working to remove the problems that face our children. Work like this, without wanting anything in return, is serving the Lord in all.

The mystics tell us that we are born for one purpose: to expand our awareness until we see everyone on the face of the earth as our very own, our kith and kin. Distant as it may sound, the joy of this all-embracing love is within the reach of us all, and we don't have to wait until the afterlife to taste it. Every step along the way brings greater happiness, love, and richness to life.

More than three thousand years ago, sages who belong not just to India but to the whole world gave us one of the

earliest spiritual treasures known to history, the Rig Veda.
Listen to a prayer addressed to all of us:

> Meet together, talk together.
> May your minds comprehend alike.
> Common be your action and achievement,
> Common be your thoughts and intentions,
> Common be the wishes of your heart,
> So there may be thorough union among you.

Unity is strength; unity is the purpose of love. In relationships it may begin with physical expression, but holding hands and dancing cheek to cheek is just the surface of
love. Two hearts becoming one, two lives becoming one:
that is the meaning of love. We just don't know the sig-
nals. We don't know the code.

But Francis broke the code; Teresa of Avila deciphered
its signs. Teresa said, *"Amor saca amor."* Love begets
love. When we give love, we draw love to us from everyone around us, and in that love is the highest heaven a
human being can know. When you give yourself to all,
the mystics say, you no longer love just one person here
and another there; you become love itself.

This is a heavenly insight into the depths of the human
heart. We begin by loving just one or two people, but the
day will come when we catch the entire world in our love.
Imagine the joy of loving all creatures, all people, the
whole of nature! As the Upanishads say, everywhere such
a person goes, he or she is at home in a compassionate
universe:

> Those who see all creatures in themselves
> And themselves in all creatures know no fear.
> Those who see all creatures in themselves
> And themselves in all creatures know no grief.
> How can the multiplicity of life
> Delude the one who sees its unity?

CHAPTER 5
Patience

*Blessed are they that mourn, for they shall be
comforted.*

YEARS AGO MY WIFE AND I went for a walk in a
particularly lovely part of Berkeley, high in the hills on
the fringes of Tilden Park. Now and then through the lush
greenery we glimpsed a breathtaking panorama of San
Francisco Bay. The homes there in the Berkeley hills,
built over shady ravines filled with manzanita and bay
laurel trees and alive with the song of birds, are handsome
and costly. Many of them probably represent the lifetime
efforts of their owners, who have managed to surround
themselves with beauty and an enviable measure of pri-
vacy.

But as we looked out across the bay toward San
Francisco and the Golden Gate, we saw a curious brown
layer of air. Even at this height, auto and industrial fumes
had spoiled the atmosphere so much that my eyes were
smarting. And on every lot I saw a sign prominently dis-
played: "Property Protected by Burglar Alarm System."

Fortunate as these homeowners are, they have not managed to escape the problems of pollution and crime that we have created for ourselves as a society.

Moreover, the security these homes afford is limited at best. Visible a little higher up the hill were charred tree stumps and a lone chimney, grim reminders of a grass fire that had swept the hills a few years earlier, sparing these particular houses at the instance of a chance shift in the wind. Like an ironic comment on the whole scene, someone's burglar alarm whined on in the distance, triggered perhaps by a wandering cat.

I wonder if there is anyone who has not dreamed at some time of devising a perfect world, a never-never land where no sorrow can intrude. We may not realize it, but most of us cling to this dream in our heart of hearts. Even while we are working and saving for that storybook home in the perfect neighborhood, I suspect, what lingers stubbornly at the back of our mind is the story of Shangri-La, the hidden city of perfection untouched by tears and time.

Not only the pursuit of wealth and possessions, but many of our other activities as well stem ultimately from the desire to isolate ourselves from sorrow. Even immersing ourselves in hobbies, intellectual pursuits, or relationships can be attempts to create a little world where beauty and harmony are permanent, where disorder and distress cannot enter. We can spend the better part of our lives attempting to construct the perfect personal environment, a kind of bubble that will insulate us against everything that is unpleasant. But sorrow is woven into the very texture of life. Pain, disappointment, depression, illness, bereavement, a sense of inadequacy in our work or our relationships . . . the list could go on and on. "Dispose all things according to your will and judgment," says Thomas a Kempis; "you will always find that of necessity you must suffer somewhat, either willingly or against your will; and so you shall always find the Cross."

Is there meaning in this pattern, in the inescapable mingling of sorrow and joy? The mystics say there is. If tears are a fact of life, they have several lessons to teach us, and the first is to learn to keep on an even keel through life's inevitable storms. When we master this skill, a good deal of personal sorrow falls away. "Life will always be full of ups and downs," my grandmother used to say. "But you don't have to go up and down with them. You can teach your mind to be calm and kind whatever comes."

Meister Eckhart, when asked by his close friends to leave them a message that would sum up all he had ever said, replied:

> Some people want to recognize God only in some pleasant enlightenment, and then they get pleasure and enlightenment but not God. Somewhere it is written that God shines in the darkness where every now and then we get a glimpse of him. More often, God is where his light is least apparent. Therefore we ought to expect God in all manners and all things evenly. . . .
>
> Someone may now say: I should be glad to look for God evenly in all shapes and things, but my mind does not always work that way. . . . To which I reply: That is too bad! . . . Whatever the way that leads you most frequently to awareness of God, follow that way. . . . But it would be nobler and better to achieve rest and security through evenness, by which one might take God and enjoy him in any manner, in any thing, and not have to delay and hunt around for your special way. That has been my joy.

Imagine the immense security of what Eckhart describes: to "take God and enjoy him in any manner, in any thing"! Evenness of mind in any situation; the ability to enjoy life thoroughly when everything about you is going wrong, and to remain steady, loving, and creative even when tragedy strikes. Meditation is a tool that can enable us to do just that – to keep the mind on an even keel under all circumstances. And the benefits flow both ways: the more steady you can keep your mind during the day, the deeper your meditation will be.

The Mind and Stress

Training the mind to stay steady brings another precious benefit: it protects us from the physiological impact of negative emotions and stress.

There is plenty of evidence today to suggest that destructive mental states like anger, depression, anxiety, and resentment have a serious impact on physical health. The medical sciences have made tremendous strides in the past century, yet I have no doubt that meditation will prove as important as medicine in keeping the body well. The function of meditation is twofold: it calms and slows the mind, and by driving the words of an inspirational passage deep into consciousness, it gradually transforms corrosive negative emotions into positive states of mind which release vitality and spread a protective shield against the stress of life.

Some of the most interesting insights in medicine concern what appears to be almost an epidemic of stress-related disorders. We reassure ourselves that the infectious diseases that plagued past centuries have been brought under control, some even wiped off the face of the globe; yet if medical experts from another age were to observe us today, they might comment, "The job is not yet done. So far, your industrial progress has traded one kind of epidemic for another." I have read estimates that two thirds of the people who seek help from family physicians suffer from conditions arising out of stress. There is evidence that stress is a major risk factor in six of the worst killers in modern industrial societies: cardiovascular disease, cancer, pulmonary disease, cirrhosis of the liver, accidents, and suicide.

Dr. Herbert Benson, professor of medicine at the

Harvard Medical School, is one of the most respected of the thousands of physicians who maintain that traditional efforts are no longer adequate to deal with the stress of modern life. Dr. Benson recommends meditation as "a natural antidote to tension." He and dedicated associates like Joan Borysenko have done important work in exploring how what he calls "the relaxation response" – essentially, repetition of a mantram in the mind for a short period once or twice a day – can be used as therapy for relieving stress. This kind of work may go a long way toward preventing some of the major health problems of our times.

But as stress researchers realize, full health is more than just the absence of disease. It means a dynamic harmony of body and mind which allows us to live at our full physical, emotional, and spiritual potential. In this state of "full wellness," stress is not merely something to cope with. As Dr. Hans Selye put it, stress is really "the spice of life." Trying to avoid stressful events, Dr. Selye says, will not help us to improve our emotional health. Instead of trying simply to survive stress, we should aim at flourishing under it, making use of anything life brings. Translated into spiritual terms, that is precisely the ideal Meister Eckhart gave us: "evenness, by which one might take God and enjoy him in any manner, in any thing."

To attain this state, we need a way to get deep into consciousness where the emotions and perceptions that make life stressful arise. When meditation penetrates below the surface of consciousness, as in sustained concentration on an inspirational passage, it becomes more rejuvenation than relaxation. By transforming negative states of mind, it actually guards us against destructive thinking habits, which makes it invaluable simply as health insurance. My own belief, based on decades of observation, is that this kind of meditation not only confers a measure of resistance against some serious ailments, but also releases the inner resources to function vigorously and effectively right into the evening of life.

On one point, medical science and mysticism concur without question: we have no way to rid life of unfortunate events; a minimum of stress is part of the human condition. This is the stress that we can learn to thrive on.

Beyond that minimum, however, there are kinds of stress that we impose on ourselves by our own ways of thinking, both individually and as a society. These sources of stress may be difficult to get rid of, but they are not ordained by fate or God. They are consequences of human choices, and when they impose a severe toll on health and happiness, there is no virtue at all in learning to live with them. In fact, learning to live with them may sometimes mean learning to die with them.

In this class fall some of the most deep rooted consequences of our industrial civilization and its values: stressors like polluted air, food, and water; urban violence; and the ever-present threat of nuclear war. Other causes come from personal ways of thinking, which shape our behavior and decisions: the kind of work we do, where and how we do it, where we live, how we spend our leisure time. All of these show an intimate connection between the way we think and the sources of sorrow in our lives. To give just one instance, a recent survey disclosed that people who live close to the Los Angeles International Airport have a much higher rate of hypertension and heart disease than those who live in a quieter environment. For many people, as one of the directors of a major stress institute points out, the principal source of stress in their lives is their life-style itself.

This kind of stress *is* avoidable, even if the cost is a less lucrative job or a lot of time and effort spent on making changes in City Hall. But it is important to understand that even if we do everything we can think of to remove outside sources of stress from our lives – even if, like

Ronald Colman in the movie *Lost Horizon*, we can somehow find our way to Shangri-La – stress will still pose a
threat because its principal source is the mind. A person
whose mind is well trained can manage in the midst of a
stressful environment. Noise and pollution will take their
toll on the body, but vitality and resistance will remain
high. By contrast, a person whose mind is out of control
can suffer from stress while lying on a quiet beach in Saint-
Tropez.

On the whole, Americans are exceptionally concerned
about their health. Yet most of us give ninety-nine percent
of our attention to caring for the body and almost nothing
to preventive care for the mind. Three of the most widely
prescribed drugs in our country today are Inderal for hypertension, Tagamet for ulcer or hiatal hernia, and Valium
for agitation. This is the only treatment most of us know.
I am not saying that these drugs are not useful under the
guidance of a skilled physician, but I do not believe that
drugs can ever get at the emotional components of such
conditions. All they can do, which is helpful but not healing, is control symptoms. For healing, what is required is
much more sweeping: not only changes in life-style but
changes in thought-style. You can eat a perfectly balanced
diet, sleep at night on the lullaby of a waterbed, and
homestead in the most remote of woods, but if your
thoughts do not obey you, you will still be subject to
stress.

As long as we are resentful, for example, stress *has* to
dog our footsteps. It is the same with jealousy, anxiety,
impatience, depression, and anger. Researchers are only
beginning to trace the steps by which these states of mind
subject the body to stress. But whatever the mechanisms,
it seems clear that the physical symptoms of stress will not
vanish until we learn to control the states of mind that
bring them on.

At present, researchers in these areas have naturally

tended to concentrate on particular emotional states. To what kind of stress does anger subject the body? What, if any, are the physical effects of chronic anxiety or low self-esteem? These are fascinating questions, but one unsuspected connection that I would like to see explored has more to do with the underlying dynamics of the mind, regardless of the specific emotions involved: what stress is imposed by a mind that is excitable, prone to race off at the slightest provocation when events or people do not behave the way they "should"?

By now, researchers generally acknowledge that it is not so much events that subject us to stress as the way we perceive and interpret those events. Richard Lazarus of the University of California at Berkeley, for example, defines stress as a "relationship between the person and the environment that is *appraised by the person* as taxing or exceeding his or her resources and endangering his or her well-being." (The emphasis is mine.) Put simply, if we interpret an event as threatening, the body responds to what the mind warns is a stressful situation. But if we see the same event as challenging, bodily responses may actually be enhanced.

My submission is that those whose minds are prone to race off in any kind of conditioned response to life's ups and downs – whatever the cause, whatever the response – are going to be subject to stress everywhere they go, simply because the mind is constantly subjecting the body to physiological arousal. By contrast, those who know how to keep their mind on an even keel will respond to life's challenges with calmness, alertness, and even eagerness. Events that others call stressful will be, for them as for Dr. Selye, "the spice of life." I want to emphasize this conclusion, because it differs significantly from current thinking. What makes the difference is not personality type but evenness of mind – which is a skill that anyone can learn.

Excitement and Depression

Paradoxically, it is the mystics – supposedly babes in the woods where the affairs of the world are concerned – who give us the most practical insights into how to stay even through life's ups and downs. And one of the most surprising of these insights seems almost a paradox itself: if you want to teach your mind to stay even, the time to practice is not so much when fortune frowns as when fortune smiles.

Keeping even minded is difficult enough in unpleasant situations, when the mind strains to race off in anger or fear. But keeping calm in the face of excitement is even harder. Pleasure makes the mind race too, but because it is pleasant, our natural response is to sit back and enjoy the ride. Why not? The problem is that if you let your mind race in pleasant situations, you will not be able to keep it from speeding out of control in anger, fear, or some kind of compulsive behavior. If you want your mind to listen to you at such times, you have to keep it steady always.

Here the mystics give priceless and thoroughly misunderstood advice. When something exciting comes, they say, don't get excited. Put up with it. Soon it will be over.

This kind of advice is as welcome as a wet blanket. Everybody wants pleasure, and if it comes rarely, the least we should be able to do is enjoy it when it comes. But the mystics are not really trying to bleach the joy out of life. They are sharing the real secret of enjoyment. How can you enjoy anything, they ask, without peace of mind? It is one of life's most basic questions. Happiness requires a calm observer. When the mind gets speeded up, it is moving too fast to sit back and observe quietly, "Ah, that's good!" What the mystics are telling us is "Go ahead and enjoy; just don't get excited about it." Joy and excitement are two different things. William Blake captured the secret in well-known lines:

> He who binds to himself a joy
> Doth the winged life destroy.
> But he who kisses the joy as it flies
> Lives in Eternity's sunrise.

Actually, as your thinking slows down through the influence of meditation, excitement as such will lose its appeal. Nobody really enjoys a jangled nervous system; it is simply because of past conditioning that we confuse jangle with joy. For me today, any kind of excitement would be an unwelcome intrusion, because the still mind is so full of love and joy. Getting excited over something pleasant would be most unpleasant, because my heart is already full.

One possible connection between stress and illness is that psychologiscal stress drains energy – energy that the body needs to stay vital, resist disease, and heal. Emotional storms – in fact, any kind of excitement – consume a tremendous amount of personal energy, which cannot help taking a toll on the nervous system – and, I suspect, on the circulatory and immune systems as well.

By nature, an untrained mind is excitement-prone, always ready to pick up some hitchhiking thought that promises to add interest to the ride. What happens is that the hitchhiker decides where to go. No wonder we find our mind out of gas toward the end of the day! It has been driving around and around, here and there, looking for joy in all the wrong places, and when we try to get started the next morning, we need some kind of psychic auto club to come out with a can of gas. We can sample all the medicines on the druggist's shelves, exercise like an Olympic champion, resort to the latest that medical technology can offer; no physical regimen can counteract the energy-wasting habits of the mind.

When I first moved to Berkeley, I was surprised to see the parade of hitchhikers that used to gather along University Avenue just where it joins the freeway. Most of them were thoughtful enough to carry signs to let you know just where they wanted to go. Compulsive thoughts carry signs too. We are going along, intent on our business, when some tempting thought standing just within our field of vision raises a sign saying "Excitement!" We think, "Great!" Who wouldn't pull off the road to give that hitchhiker a ride? Doesn't excitement mean pleasure? We get so enticed by the very thought of it that we don't think to look at what is printed on the back of the sign: "WARNING: this fellow may be hazardous to your security. Emotional turmoil, sleepless nights, and long-term frustration may result." He says he's going to Excitement, but the real destination is Depression.

Whatever our past conditioning, whatever our present state of mind, none of us is compelled to go on picking up excitement every time it sticks out its thumb. Every one of us has the freedom to drive by without a glance. That is the kind of training that meditation and the mantram can give your mind. If you don't put your foot on the brake, pull over, open the car door, and let excitement in, your mind is not going to be affected by it: which means that to the same degree, it will not be affected by fear, depression, anxiety, anger, jealousy, and any number of the other unpleasant states of mind that tie the stomach in knots during the day and turn our nights to nightmares.

I read recently that an estimated twenty to thirty million Americans are subject to serious depression. One glossy drug advertisement describes the symptoms in catchy language: "Depression. It can affect you in ways you would never suspect. Unexplainable jumpiness or anxiety. Unusual irritability. Sleep disturbances. Difficulty in concentrating or remembering. Physical pains that are hard to pin down. Appetite loss (or overeating). A loss of interest or pleasure in your job, family life, hobbies or sex. A downhearted period that gets worse and just won't go away. Frequent or unexplainable crying spells.

A loss of self-esteem or an attitude of indifference. A combination of the above symptoms, persisting for two weeks or more, can be an indication of depressive illness and a warning to seek the advice of a doctor. . . . "

Feelings like these are all too familiar in today's world, and no one should feel guilty or inadequate if they strike home. Depression is built into our very way of life. Everywhere the media promise us happiness, pleasure, leisure, fulfillment, luxury. We want to be happy and are taught to be excited; we want to love and be loved, to cherish and be cherished, and are told we will find what we are looking for in sex. We are promised the right to have our own way, encouraged to believe that our first responsibility is to ourselves; yet somehow our relationships don't seem to thrive. More and more frequently we may look around and wonder what we are living for; life seems such a dull, meaningless round.

These are not matters of right and wrong; this is simply the dynamics of the mind. Our way of life puts the mind on a roller coaster with no seat belt, and the faster it goes, the sooner it gets jaded. One minute it is flying toward the sky, shrieking, "I'm high!" But the next minute it is hurtling down, and life seems hopeless. That is the nature of the mind: it never stops moving, and when it goes up, it has to come down. If we could interview the mind on "Sixty Minutes" and demand, "Why do you keep causing all this trouble?" it would shrug and reply, "That's how I am. I'm fickle by nature."

Human beings do not need excitement; they need meaning, purpose, a higher goal and some way of getting there. Without these, for those who are sensitive, life may soon lose its value.

Meditation is such a powerful shield that it can make the mind depression-proof, simply by slowing it down. The slower the mind, the steadier it has to be, and the less susceptible to excitement. When your meditation is going well, nothing that happens will be able to disturb your peace of mind.

By and large, meditation is a preventive measure. The time to guard yourself against depression is before you get depressed, and nothing provides a better shield than training the mind. I want to make it very clear, however, that in extreme cases, meditation should not be initiated as treatment. For those who suffer from life-threatening depression, or who are taking antidepressive drugs under a doctor's supervision, it may even be dangerous. If you are in this category, please do not jump into meditation without the close guidance of an experienced teacher. But there *is* a powerful spiritual tool which offers safe, fast help for anyone in times of crisis: repetition of the mantram.

In times of distress, when you try to call up the Holy Name, you may have difficulty even remembering how it goes. Your attention will be caught in your own turmoil, and every time you try to draw it back, it will rebel and slip away again. Here is where toughness comes in. No matter how many times you have to try, just keep bringing your attention back to the Holy Name again and again until your mind is calm.

When the weight of mental anguish is especially heavy, it can keep the mind from resting even at night. Here again, the best recourse is the Holy Name. Sleep does not come gradually. It falls like a curtain, and between the last waking moment and the first sleeping moment, there is an arrow's entry into deeper consciousness. If you can keep repeating the mantram until you fall asleep in it, the mantram will slip into the depths of your consciousness and work its healing wonders even in your sleep. When you are tormented by bad dreams, the Holy Name will come like a nurse to assuage your fears.

Guarding the mind against excitement is in no way attempting to run away from life. It is telling life quietly, "I am not afraid of you. I don't ask for any favors." You will never catch me holding out my hat to life and saying, "Please, I beg you, give me a few things that I like. You can put in one or two surprises if you care to, but only if they are pleasant. Don't put in anything that I don't like." This kind of begging is beneath our dignity as human beings.

Imagine getting up in the morning not even bothering to ask, "Are people going to like me? Are people going to dislike me? Are things going to go my way? Will I get jobs that I enjoy doing?" If you ask at all, it will only be to wonder, "Will I get a chance to help others?" If you do, it will not matter if you like or dislike what you have to do, or whether those around you will like you or not. All that is important is that you can make a contribution; that is what gives life meaning and value.

Even where food is concerned, you can train your mind not to get excited when things you like or dislike come. Food is a perfect training ground for the mind. I don't go in for ascetic fare; I enjoy everything I eat. But I eat only food that is wholesome and nourishing, and I never eat just to enjoy. If my life is a trust, I want everything I eat to help me live longer and work harder for the benefit of others. Whether it is food or exercise or entertainment – all of which have an important place in spiritual living – the question I ask is not "Do I like this?" but "Will this add to my capacity to give?" When your mind has been trained like this, there can never be any question of depression.

"Hurry Sickness"

Today's mania for speed strikes right at the root of our capacity for an even mind. How often we find ourselves locked into behavior and situations that force us to hurry, hurry, hurry! By now, with so much publicity given to Type A behavior, most of us are aware that compulsive speed – "hurry sickness" – is one component of a personality that puts us at risk for heart disease. But hurry has another alarming repercussion that is less suspected: it cripples patience, which is vital for learning to steady the mind in times of trial.

A few months ago my wife and I drove to San Francisco for a movie. We got there early – one of my favorite ways of not getting pressured by time – so after we got our tickets, we decided to take a short walk. We were about to cross a busy street when a car stalled at the intersection next to us. The light turned green, and the driver of the car behind leaned on his horn. Nothing unusual; just another noisy incident in city life.

But the first driver did not simply sit and continue to crank his engine. In an instant he had burst out of his car with a snarl and was trying to drag the other driver through the window. Before we realized what was happening, they were scuffling like animals.

Fortunately a third party in the car intervened, and after more honking the intersection was cleared without injury. But if one of those men had had a gun, I realized, I might have witnessed not just a fight but a murder – all because of hurry, and the habit of getting excited when things don't go our way.

It shows how far we have traveled from patience when a few moments' delay, a trivial disappointment, an unexpected obstacle, makes a man explode in anger. Hurry makes a calm mind impossible: and without peace of mind, how can we enjoy anything, from a movie to good health? As for having things work out just how and when we want, wisdom demands that we learn to expect the unexpected. Life thinks nothing of making changes in our plans – after all, it has a lot of people in the picture. If we take personally every disruption of our schedule, we will go about feeling insecure most of the time.

In other words, patience is not only a mental virtue; it is an asset even for physical health. I'm sure you are aware of the way your heart races when you get impatient. Perhaps you have noticed, too, that your breathing becomes faster and more shallow. Doesn't it seem reasonable that if you can strengthen your patience to such a degree that other people's behavior never upsets you, your heart, lungs, and nervous system will be on vacation? Don't take my word for it; try it. At first, I agree, you will feel some stress from going against an established habit. But that is to be expected. After all, when you have been leading a sedentary life, walking only as far as the garage or the television set, it is stressful for a while to get out and jog; your heart and lungs complain. But how quickly they feel better for it! It is the same with patience; this is one of the grandest secrets of health.

Research evidence today suggests that emotional immunity to negative states of mind may well be linked to physical immunity, even resistance to disease. A person who is even minded, who doesn't get shaken if people speak ill of him or excited when they praise her to the skies – such a person, I submit, is a poor host for disease. That kind of inner toughness creates a protective buffer of what one researcher, Suzanne Kobasa, calls "hardiness": enhanced resistance to illness and the everyday stress of daily life.

So inverted are our modern values that we associate patience with passivity and admire those who bowl over their competitors in their rush to the top. The spiritual perspective turns this right side up. *La paciencia todo lo alcanza,* Saint Teresa used to repeat: "Patience attains everything." Through patience, every goal can be reached.

Teresa's language would have been appreciated by her brothers, who were conquistadors in the New World. For them, to conquer meant to impose their way on unsuspecting peoples through superior military might. But for Teresa the real battle was within, and the surest weapon against the negative forces in human consciousness is patience. Patience means self-mastery: the capacity to hold on and remain loving in a difficult situation when every atom of your being wants to turn and run.

★

Perversely, the more we try to run from occasions that might cause us grief, the more we add to our burden of it. Trying to avoid suffering only makes suffering more likely, because we become increasingly rigid about the way life has to perform to meet our requirements. Again, no one is more insightful than Thomas a Kempis:

> . . . As long as suffering seems so grievous that you desire to flee it, so long will you be ill at ease, and the desire to escape tribulation will follow you everywhere.

"The desire of escaping tribulation" is Thomas's tactful way of referring to our enslavement to personal likes and dislikes. We are held captive by so many tiny fears of life not working out: tied fast, like Gulliver, by a thousand Lilliputian cables. It's Saturday night, and you have a dinner engagement with the date of your dreams: what if the menu turns out to be uninspired? Suppose the music isn't right? And perhaps your companion is only pretending to have a good time . . . Thoughts like these run through our heads more than most people know. But if we go on worrying like this about every little unpleasant possibility, distress can follow us through life like a shadow.

How can we reverse this very natural habit of mind? By doing our best in whatever life sends without ever asking what it is going to send next. Every day brings circumstances in which we can practice this, beginning with the thousand and one little likes and dislikes that really matter very little to anybody but ourselves. By seizing every opportunity to do cheerfully things we do not like, especially when they benefit somebody else, we can gradually dissolve every fetter of anxiety about life's challenges. Slowly we begin to sit up straight, rub our aching arms and legs with indescribable relief, and wonder how we ever thought we enjoyed being tied down.

"Tribulation" is an old-fashioned word, but it describes rather accurately the day-in, day-out endeavor that is the real substance of spiritual living. It starts at the breakfast table – staying cheerful, not hiding behind the news-paper, listening with attention as your son recounts every play in last night's soccer match. It goes on at the office, where you try for the hundredth time to reconcile two co-workers who are allergic to each other. It continues late into the afternoon, when a missing file threatens to close your promising career. And after work, commute traffic is so torturous that if there were a muscle where patience is exercised, it would be swollen and throbbing by the time you pull in the driveway.

But there you are, as relaxed as if you had spent the day on a putting green! To look at you no one would guess that inside, you are toe to toe with a relentless adversary: self-will. And you are holding your own.

What makes us impatient? The mystics give a good, scientific answer: acts of impatience, repeated over and over and over. Then how do we make ourselves more patient? By trying to be more patient every day. When we meditate on passages like the Prayer of Saint Francis, the muscles of the mind, which at present may be so flabby that they can hardly bear the weight of any sorrow, grow stronger and more resilient every day. Every provocation is an opportunity. If we do everything we can every day to stretch our patience, one day it is going to be inex-haustible.

A few days ago I was in the grocery store watching an exasperated young mother contend with her little one. Hitching a ride on the shopping cart, he seemed deter-mined to throw in all the items advertised on television;

unfortunately, his fancies did not coincide with his mother's notions of nutrition. After she had taken out half a dozen items and set them back on the shelves, she announced for half the store to hear: "Patrick, there's a limit!"

Every parent can sympathize with her situation. But I wish I had been able to tell her on the spot something the mystics have proven to us with their very lives: There really is *no* limit. There is no limit to the patience we can develop, no end to our capacity for bearing with the sorrow that life impartially doles out.

This is a crucial issue. No matter how hard we try, aren't there occasions when we are bound to blow up at *some*one – our partner, our neighbor, our children, our mother-in-law? It grieves us to realize that even with our loved ones, we cannot always control our own temper. Sometimes it breaks loose and runs amok almost with a will of its own.

It is precisely at such a moment, when your temper is about to burst all bounds, that love for the Lord can come to your rescue – and the rescue of those around you. If God is the furthest thing from your mind, that is where toughness comes in. Go for a walk and start repeating the Holy Name for all you're worth – not aloud but in your mind – and keep bringing your attention back to it over and over again until your mind is calm. Then, when you go back to the scene that brought you distress, you will be able to stay relatively calm and compassionate. You can speak kindly, even when the other person's response is far from kind. If you have a very personal relationship with the Lord, you may feel almost as if a loving arm has slipped around you and set you back on firm ground. This security – knowing that the loving arm is always ready – is what makes for joy.

Remember, though, that in repeating the Holy Name like this, you are not appealing to somebody on high. You are asking the Lord who lives in the depths of your heart, "Please give me more patience, more endurance to bear this cheerfully. Release the strength I need to stand firm, so that I can help those around me to stand firm too." The mantram invariably brings help, but help always comes from within – even when it rises from recesses beyond the reach of our small, personal self.

The key here is detachment – not from others but from ourselves, from our own self-centered insistence on getting things the way we want. With detachment, life's ups and downs need hardly affect our security at all.

Meditation and the mantram clear our eyes so we can see when purely personal motives are coming into play. The mind, remember, can present us with only a fragmentary picture, never a faithful representation of the whole. When we get deep below the surface of consciousness in meditation, the mind becomes still and clear. Then we can see for ourselves to what extent our mind has distorted the picture we have of even the people closest to us. With that insight, much of what seems to threaten and distress us dissolves.

All of us, of course, believe we are the never-ending stream of thoughts that is our mind. But just as there are hurricanes and earthquakes in the world outside us, there are emotional typhoons and tremors deep in the caverns of consciousness, and this turmoil is constantly shaping and reshaping our thoughts. As long as we believe we are these thoughts, how can we avoid being shaken and blown off course by such violent disturbances?

Gradually, in meditation, our thoughts slow down further and further, until we are able to see that these storms of the mind are not who we are. We need not be blown about by emotional hurricanes; we can watch winds like anger rising, just as a veteran meteorologist would, noting changes but not getting entangled – that is, without feeling any compulsion to act on them. No one can imagine what an era of freedom this ushers in. It is not that turmoil will vanish: causing us trouble sometimes is in the nature of people, just as it is in our nature to cause trouble sometimes to others. But when the mind quiets down and we see more clearly, we gain faith that we have the inner resources to stay calm and kind no matter what circumstances come our way. With that, a good deal of life's burden of personal sorrow is lifted.

★

But sorrow is more than something to be endured. It can be an invaluable teacher. You must have seen those highway signs warning, "Go Back. Wrong Way!" Where roads are concerned, we all understand this warning and know we should turn around. If only we could understand life's signs so easily! Sorrow is often a warning with the same message: "Go back. Change your direction. You are going the wrong way."

Every creature is conditioned to avoid pain; this is a built-in safety mechanism to protect our bodies from harm. When you eat more than you should, for example, you should feel reassured if your stomach aches. Your body is telling you in the only language it knows, "Please don't do this again; it's not good for me."

Similarly, mental and emotional suffering often comes as the consequence of our own thoughts and actions. Trying to hide from suffering, closing our eyes to it, means we will go on repeating the same mistakes, making the suffering worse.

When you find your mind in turmoil, when you begin to feel that you are not worth much and your life is a waste, it is time to make a U-turn. Otherwise, sorrow will only increase. So when pain comes, don't shrink away from it; that will only hurt you more. When you feel threatened, don't hide or put up hostile defenses; that will only wound you more. Try to keep your mind steady, drawing on the mantram and meditation: if there is a lesson to be learned, it will sink in. All of us have this choice. And once you have learned how to keep your mind still, you will act only from love and live only in love, which means that personal sorrow will be erased from your life. That is the purpose of pain: to urge us toward the discovery that love, joy, meaning, and peace of mind can be found only in living for all.

Most of us, as my grandmother once told me bluntly, confuse self-pity and grief. Granny was as tough as she was loving. When I would come to her crying because my feelings were hurt, she could be terribly unsympathetic. "That's not grief," she would say. "You're just feeling sorry for yourself." Self-pity weakens us; grief, which means sorrow for others, ennobles us and releases inner resources to help.

It requires detachment and a measure of self-understanding to know when the mind is just reciting its favorite litany of "Poor me, nobody cares for me, nobody loves me." Part of the strategy is never to ask who loves you; instead, ask how you can love more.

I used to teach classes in Shakespeare in my university days, and I always remember King Lear's tragic question to his daughters: "How much do you love me? How much do you love me? How much do you love me?" Cordelia, who loved him truly, could not adorn her answer with flowery phrases, and her father flew into a rage that turned to hatred. Such acute self-will and self-pity cannot help leading to tragedy, and toward the end of the play we see Lear standing on a desolate moor, abandoned by all but those he has himself abandoned, raising his arms to the stars in despair and crying, "Look upon a man as full of grief as he is of age!"

If I were to write a play on the same subject, I would have King Lear tell his daughters, "I don't care whether you love me; I will never ask. Love is not a contract. Love

me or hate me, my life will be devoted to you always."
The end of the play would be magnificent: Lear standing
as majestic as a real king should and saying to the heavens,
"Look upon a man as full of joy as he is of love."

Sorrow is an essential part of living: not good, not
something to be courted or embraced, just unavoidable.
But in facing sorrow we have a choice, and wherever there
is choice there is freedom. "Pain is an enemy," goes an Indian proverb, "only when we do not welcome it as a
friend." Sorrow is a teacher whose lesson is to go beyond
sorrow. No one likes heartburn, but we can learn from
the experience that there is a limit to how much ice cream
can satisfy. In the same way, we can learn from heartbreak
not to clutch for happiness at any thing or person outside
us.

Yet the tragicomedy of sorrow is that most of us go into
the same situation again and again and still do not learn.
This is the illusion that Indian mysticism calls *maya*. It always reminds me of the old shell game, which I used to see
in my village in South India. No matter how many times
we fail to guess which coconut shell covers the rupee, we
are always ready to try just one more time.

In the end, sorrow comes simply from asking of life
what it cannot give. As long as we believe ourselves to be
physical creatures, there has to be suffering when we
pursue our desires. Asking material things and outward
activities to satisfy the spirit, to borrow an old Persian
saying, is like asking an elephant to satisfy its hunger with
a sesame seed.

Initiation into universal consciousness, it has been said,
is initiation into universal empathy . . . and therefore
into universal sorrow. As love deepens, unseen walls that
isolate us from others begin to melt away. No longer can
we pick up a newspaper and read about the hungry and
homeless without feeling ourselves intimately involved.
No longer can we watch passively as violence rages in

Central America. That suffering will be our suffering, and it will change our lives: we will take time and resources from other activities and find ways to help. Spiritual growth means a heightened sense of sorrow, but it also brings the inner resources we need to help assuage that sorrow: strength, insight, compassion, creative action.

Opportunities for becoming more aware of the needs of others lie all around us. Helping is the true vocation of every human being, and we don't have to wait for some terrible event to come and reveal it to us. A neighbor's wife is ill – why not offer to take her children for the day? Your daughter has come home from school in tears again: you can let her go her own way, or you can rearrange your schedule and make time to listen and help. Little things, all of them, but they add up to works of love.

Most of us, at least at the beginning, can shoulder only a little burden of such sorrow at a time. Yet by the end of a day, when everything is tallied, we may find we have lifted a hefty load. Miraculously enough, we will not feel the fatigue we used to feel when our sorrows were strictly personal. In this way, even in our own rather pedestrian lives, we discover the truth of what Jesus promised: "My yoke is easy, and my burden light."

Which lover of God has not had to face mighty storms? Name anyone you like; you will find that suffering seemed to seek that person out. Can we expect divine love to come any more easily to us? Which of us would learn to be selfless if life were one long pleasure cruise? For the aspiring lover of God, stressful situations become fuel to "the fire of the soul" which consumes our ugliest, most selfish tendencies and fans the spark of divinity in us into flame. It may sound impossible, but we can cultivate the same eagerness to face every challenge to spiritual growth.

CHAPTER 6
Love

*Blessed are they that are persecuted for
righteousness' sake, for theirs is the kingdom
of heaven.*

COMING FROM SOUTH INDIA, I never saw snow
until I was sixteen. Not only that, I had never even seen
people who had seen snow. When I came to this country
on the Fulbright exchange program, I explained to the au-
thorities that I was accustomed to a mild climate. The
State Department thoughtfully posted me to the University of Minnesota.

It was there that I heard about skiing. Ski enthusiasts, I
discovered, have to get up even earlier to go skiing than I
do for meditation. "You have to drive all the way to the
mountains," friends explained, "and then get in line for
the lift." And that is only the beginning of the discomfort.
"Look at all that gear you have to carry and put on!" I
teased them. "Not the least of which are those two long
fiberglass appendages that to me are only impediments to
movement. And then standing about for hours in the
snow . . . "

"You don't know the joys of skiing," my friends retorted. "When you're shooting down a fast, powdery slope, you're not a groundling any more; you're a bird in flight. The weight of your body just falls away." "The same thing happens to me every morning in meditation," I said. "Only with one big difference: wouldn't you find it more challenging to ski *up* the slopes?"

That really got them interested. Imagine starting from the Rhine valley and skiing straight up the Matterhorn! That is the challenge of the spiritual life, the greatest challenge you can imagine: skiing *up* the slopes of life, against all the downward pull of physical and emotional conditioning. To attain any worthwhile goal, even in sports, don't we have to overcome certain obstacles? Isn't a measure of pain part of the effort? It is the same with living in heaven here on earth, winning that "pearl of great price." There, too, we have to endure what it costs to overcome the obstacles in our way; but just as in skiing, if our desire is deep enough, what seems like pain to the rest of the world is dwarfed in comparison with the glory of our goal.

What sounds like a negative note in this beatitude is really proof of the depth and breadth of Jesus' universal vision. If suffering is part of entering the kingdom of heaven within, it is not because life is perverse but because living in heaven means mastering a whole new way of thinking. Remember Eckhart's words: "He who would be what he ought to be must stop being what he is." When life sends us treatment that seems unfair, sometimes at the hands of those dear to us, it is not just "trial and tribulation." These are the opportunities every human being needs for cultivating the divine love that shines alike on all, without question of right or reason or favor, "that we may be the children of our Father which is in heaven: for he maketh his sun to rise on the evil as on the good, and sendeth rain on the just as on the unjust."

Every normal human being throws up his hands at this and says, "I simply am not capable of behaving like that!" Jesus assures us emphatically: You *are* capable of behaving like that. Everyone is, simply by virtue of being human; for whatever our failings, whatever our limitations, the Lord lives in every heart. I am not idealizing here. I know how difficult this can be. But when someone offends you, instead of thinking over and over again, "She hurt me! She hurt me!" you can actually use the Holy Name as an eraser. All the power behind your anger then goes into the erasing, and resentment goes no deeper than writing on water. The secret of the mind is that it is a sponge: we slowly become what we soak our consciousness in. When your mind dwells on jealousy, you cannot help becoming more jealous. When it dwells on wrongs you have suffered, you are soaking yourself in anger. The only alternative is to teach the mind to soak itself in love, through the practice of meditation and repetition of the Holy Name.

Friends often lament, "But there just doesn't seem to be any end to the negative thoughts that come up! No matter how I try to be positive and forgiving, there's always something just around the corner to upset me again. I'm not sure you realize how much negativity the ordinary person has to deal with." I assure them that indeed I do understand. That is why I know that love requires a center within oneself which nothing can shake – a sanctum sanctorum into which we can always retire to renew our strength and security. That is the purpose of meditation.

*

Again, because there is so much misunderstanding about suffering and spirituality, I find it helpful to look at the actual dynamics of the mind.

Mystics of all religions remind us that this life on earth is woven of opposites that are inseparable twins: pain and pleasure, sickness and health, praise and censure, defeat and success, birth and death. One minute people are handing us bouquets of roses; the next minute they are lobbing rotten eggs. If we function well only when people are kind to us, we are living only part-time. Love is a full-time occupation, a continuous state of mind.

We may not feel the need for approval as acutely as a movie star I read about who, in order to fall asleep at night, had to switch on a tape of her audience applauding. Yet almost all of us suffer when we are criticized, or when friends suddenly turn on us or let us down. By using blows such as these as opportunities to keep our mind steady, we can erase negative responses like depression and resentment from our hearts completely. And when all resentment, all ill will, all depression is gone, we live in heaven here on earth. Instead of looking at difficulties as deprivations, we can learn to recognize them as opportunities for deepening and widening our love. You don't run away from opportunities; you keep on the lookout for them. Lashing out at others, trying to "get even" when people are harsh, only wastes these precious chances for growth, which can come in no other way.

Wise spiritual directors have always recognized that for the vast majority of us, the widest opportunities for this kind of growth lie hidden in the give-and-take of everyday relationships. It is here that we can find the unity between ourselves and others by removing everything that keeps us separate, which is precisely what the practice of loving means.

One profound but simple secret is that when you love someone deeply, you want to share everything with that person. If she likes the novels of Somerset Maugham, you want to read them too. If he likes baseball, you want to feel the same attraction. When you find satisfaction even in enduring the same hardships, because you would rather be together in hardship than comfortably apart, you begin to escape from the narrow prison of separateness that is the human condition. That is why, whether we know it or not, each of us longs to discover in at least one relationship the unity which underlies all life, for even a fleeting taste of this unity brings enormous joy.

"He who knoweth not love, knoweth not God," says John the Apostle, "for God is love." The words sound so ethereal that most of us cannot connect them with daily life. What, we ask, do personal relationships have to do with the divine? I would reply, It is by discovering the unity between ourselves and others – *all* others – that we find our unity with God. That is why training the mind is the nuts and bolts of religion. We don't first get to know God and then, by some miracle of grace, come to love our fellow human beings. Loving comes first: learning to love others is how we move closer to the Lord. In this sense, learning to love is practicing religion. Those who can put the welfare of others before their own small personal interests are religious, even if they would deny it. And, of course, anyone who can quote scripture chapter and verse but will not put herself out for others has yet to learn what religion means.

In one of my favorite sonnets, William Shakespeare calls love "the marriage of true minds." We are so used to thinking of love as involving bodies that hearing "marriage" together with "minds" can startle us. But this is no mere turn of phrase; it holds a kernel of subtle psychology. In any relationship in which two people can hold their minds true – to each other, to compassion, to a willingness to share in sorrow as well as joy – love cannot help blossoming. What we need in order to nurture love, then, is mental disciplines that we can use to train our minds to be true.

Mystics like Thomas a Kempis tell us that the would-be lover must be a martyr. That is not particularly effective salesmanship today, but learning to stay kind when people turn against us is the essence of training the mind to love. If we do not develop this sort of inner toughness, our love will never be strong enough to support the weight of close relationships, let alone the weight of the all-embracing love to which Jesus calls us again and again: "Be ye therefore perfect, even as your Father which is in heaven is perfect."

Tradition has it that love is blind, but just the opposite is true. Love looks only to the shining goal of union; it is lack of love that is blind. The more you love, the more clearly you see the needs of others, for you are dwelling less on your own needs and desires. You know how you feel when unkind words are directed at you; when you feel one with others, you find it impossible to strike back with unkind words when someone is rude to you. No abstruse psychology is required for understanding this, simply "Do unto others as you would have them do unto you." And, Jesus would add, do it no matter what they do unto you, even when it hurts. If we want to be in love, Thomas a Kempis tells us plainly, we have to "embrace willingly all that is hard and distasteful": not in a spirit of grim self-denial, but simply in the course of trying to put others' needs before our own. Bearing sorrow cheerfully for the sake of another is the very heart of love.

This is far from the idea of romance held by the modern world, which seems to have taken lessons from commerce in all things. Today, one unkind word can be enough to make a person bristle with hostility. One well-aimed dig and we say, "I don't want to hear any more from you for the rest of the weekend!" Set aside divine love, the mystics would say, we should not even claim to have mundane love if that is how we are going to act.

Love means that regardless of what a person does to us, we will not turn our back or move away; we will stand close and go on loving. This ubiquitous question of "Why have you done this to me?" doesn't even enter in. If you slip and hurt me, what has that to do with my love for you?

None of us, I believe, really wants to strike back at those we love. We do not really get satisfaction out of hurting people who hurt us. We have simply fallen into the habit of brooding on wrongs done to us, blowing them up to the proportions of enormous antipathies, until we finally explode.

A natural antidote to this tendency of mind is to repeat the mantram as often as we can, with as much depth of feeling as we can muster. There is no mystery about driving the Holy Name deep into the mind; it is just a matter of sincere, systematic practice. By dint of sheer persistence, making use of every odd piece of time in the midst of a very busy life, I have managed to carry the Holy Name like a lifeline down into the depths of the unconscious. If I hear even one negative phrase, the Holy Name starts up, and all the power that might have flared in animosity is harnessed to love's purposes. As Mahatma Gandhi showed, we can use this power to build bridges of understanding between those who are estranged, to light lamps of sympathy between warring communities and even nations.

In the end, personal suffering always comes from self-will. Remember that pungent phrase from the *Theologica Germanica:* "Nothing burns in hell except self-will." That leaves little room for argument. No matter how justified we may feel in getting angry, the only thing that makes us flare up is that our self-will has been violated. In the end, the whole of loving consists in removing self-will; and if we are going to choose that, we have to choose suffering, for that is what removing self-will entails.

There *is* anguish in taming selfish passions that are accustomed to riding roughshod over us. When you have been striking back at others for twenty years, it hurts to sit and listen to rude words without doing or saying anything harsh, trying to keep your mind from even thinking a mean thought, just "for righteousness' sake." The capacity to bear this pain cheerfully, knowing it will lead to greater love, is the very core of spiritual disciplines. After a while, the mystics say, you will find the fierce thrill of mastery right in that pain – just as you would in the pain of a cold ski slope or of "hitting the wall" on a marathon – as you get the taste of freedom. Goodness, says the Bhagavad Gita, "may taste bitter at first, but it is found at last to be immortal wine."

Going against the grain of self-will – the insistent, overriding drive to have our own way, whatever it may cost others – can be excruciating. Yet as Meister Eckhart says bluntly, we cannot know God until we are "stripped, cleansed, and purified." As long as there is self-will, we have no choice in whether to suffer. But we *can* choose whether our suffering is to be meaningful or meaningless. We can actually use suffering to reduce suffering, to gain a state of consciousness so grand that even a step toward it is worth the cost. We can choose to bear suffering rather than add to our burden of anger, resentment, and hostility. We can choose to suffer ourselves instead of adding to the suffering of others. This pain of purification has a purpose: to remove every obstacle between ourselves and the kingdom of heaven within.

Thomas a Kempis, then, explains this beatitude precisely. Suffering becomes sweet when we see that it removes self-will and uncovers love:

> When you come to such a degree of patience that tribulation is sweet to you, and for the love of God is savory and pleasant in your sight, then you may trust that it is well with you; . . . for you have found heaven on earth.

For everyone, there comes a turning point in spiritual striving when suffering does become sweet: not out of perversity, but because it is a necessary spur to this process of perfection. It helps to remember that nothing in personality suffers but the thick covering of selfish drives and desires that stands between us and perfect love. Having this thick covering brings suffering; getting rid of it brings suffering: but the first only ensures more suffering, whereas every step toward removing self-will means a little of our burden of sorrow has fallen away.

But at the risk of repetition, let me be clear: this is no assurance that your life will be free from grief. It is only personal sorrow that falls away. The greater your sensitivity to others, the more you will be aware of the suffering borne by those around you.

Years ago I read about a little girl whose pup was run over and who sat on the curb sobbing and sobbing. When a neighbor tried to console her she replied, "It's just like being run over myself!" That is the price of love. For those who love God, when anyone dies, a part of them dies too. In the highest sense, this is the meaning of the Passion, the reason why the Messiah was called "a man of sorrows, and acquainted with grief." Living in all, you suffer whatever they suffer. But this awareness of unity is also the source of the greatest joy, because it brings the love, compassion, and creativity to relieve suffering wherever you go.

There *is* meaning in sorrow, and when that meaning is grasped, nothing in the world is more useful for us. The key lies in recognizing that we do always have a choice: not whether we are going to suffer, but when and for what. The astonishing claim of the mystic, exemplified so beautifully in the life of Jesus, is that once we begin exerting this power to choose, our suffering can be turned into joy. Eckhart says:

> Would you know for certain whether your sufferings are your own or God's? You can tell by these signs. When you suffer for yourself, in whatever way, the suffering hurts and is hard to bear. But when you suffer for God

and God alone, your suffering hurts you not; nor will it burden you, for it is God who bears the load. Believe me, if a person were willing to suffer on account of God and of God alone, then even if he should fall prey to the collective sufferings of all the world it would not trouble him nor bow him down, for God would be the bearer of his burden.

If we want to draw closer to the spark of divine love deep within, our desire will be to suffer, as Christ did, whenever it helps to relieve the suffering of others.

Before Francis of Assisi fell in love with Christ he was a troubadour, composing and singing passionate love songs. This same depth of feeling he brought to his relationship with the Lord. So great was Francis's thirst to be united with Christ that one day toward the end of his life he knelt in prayer on the secluded heights of Mount La Verna and from the depths of his heart asked his Lord for two favors: first, that he should experience, as far as possible, the suffering Christ had endured on the cross; second, that he should feel the love for all God's creatures that had moved Christ to endure that suffering. These two, suffering and love, are the two intertwining poles of Jesus' life on earth.

After long hours of intense prayer, Francis rejoined his companions. He said nothing about his experiences; yet despite his efforts to hide himself, they saw on his palms, on the soles of his feet, and in his side the stigmata, the wounds of Christ's Passion. These he would carry, concealed from all but his closest followers, for the rest of his life.

Saint Teresa of Avila is probably best remembered for her celebration of the "mystical marriage" that takes place between the soul and Christ. "It is like rain falling from the heavens into a river or a spring," she says, ". . . or it is as if a tiny streamlet enters the sea, from which it will find no way of separating itself." But the joyous union with

Christ that she experienced, as she herself explains over and over again, was possible only because she had first united herself with his suffering.

Love Is a Skill

One simple proof of love's unbelievable power is that it is still the most longed-for commodity on earth. In an age rich in technological toys, aren't we still troubled if we have a losing record in love? Even if broken relationships and divided homes become the norm, won't we always try to have and hold something more? How much solace will we find in a fat portfolio of stocks or a warehouse of possessions? The awful truth is that no one on earth is more severely handicapped than those who are unable to love. Without love we are desperately deprived – and that may prove to be our saving grace.

Love is so exquisitely elusive. It cannot be bought, cannot be badgered, cannot be hijacked. It is available only in one rare form: as the natural response of a healthy mind and healthy heart. The only way to secure it is to heal our own mind and heart. From time to time, everyone needs to be reminded that love is not something that is up to chance or fate. It is a skill, a world-class skill of mind, which anyone can gain and everyone must work to maintain, all the more so in a world that holds so little sacred.

The mystics may know of no magic to exorcise selfish urges, but they give us powerful disciplines like meditation and the mantram with which we can learn to turn around the raw energy of negative emotions like anger, jealousy, and hate. This reversal is the whole purpose of training the mind. Harnessed for unity, that same energy is love.

The other day my wife and I were driving along a narrow coastal road when we encountered a man with a flag warning of crews busy repairing the road. Heavy rains had washed out the bank from under the asphalt, so one lane was a yawning pit with no shoulder but thin air – and, hundreds of feet below, the sea.

We sat there waiting for several minutes, unable to see what was going on. For a while it seemed that there was no one in that desolate stretch except us, the flagman, and a few cows beyond the fence at the side of the road.

Then, as if the earth itself had produced them, a stream of cars erupted from nowhere and rolled by in the other direction.

No one else in the car, I feel sure, thought anything of such an ordinary occurrence. But I immediately exclaimed, "That's just how it is in the mind!" Negative thoughts can surprise us just like that. They bunch up in the mind where we can't see them; then, without the gracious warning of a flagman, they burst in and rush through consciousness before we even realize they are coming. Whenever thinking is fast and furious, whether because of anger, fear, or some fierce desire, we have no control over what thoughts come bursting through, and very little freedom in how we respond to them either. For the time being, we are trapped in that stream of thought – which means that however we respond, the consequences of our actions are likely to be disastrous.

Once you get beneath the surface of consciousness, you begin to see and to control this kind of traffic. Eventually you can become a kind of flagman in your own subconscious, stopping thoughts with the mantram until you can let them pass by in an orderly fashion. In practical terms, this means that although your mind may still think angry thoughts, you will not get caught in them or act on them; you will have latitude for choice. It is the same with most other negative emotions: resentment, jealousy, anxiety, fear. When you enter the personal unconscious, you begin to take yourself out of the orbit of compulsive thinking – the first exhilarating step toward acting in real freedom.

Compulsive thought patterns exist only so long as we support them with our belief in their power to propel us into action. Choice is hard to exercise beneath the surface of consciousness, but choice *is* there. If we are bothered by certain thoughts, we should remind ourselves that it is we who rent out the precious space within the mind. We don't have to be afraid of compulsive thoughts if we don't welcome them. If we shut the door of the mind right in their face, they will soon tire of knocking.

The deeper realms of the unconscious, which are shared by all, can be compared to a mental atmosphere that every human being breathes. Just as the atmosphere outside us contains oxygen, hydrogen, and many other elements and compounds, the atmosphere of the unconscious contains primordial forces – desires, impulses, urges, instincts – that are part of the collective record of our evolutionary past. And just as chemicals in the air around us can bring on ailments like cancer, there are thoughts in the unconscious which can pollute our inner atmosphere and bring on illness in mind and even body. If for no other reason than our own health, we need to develop our own stringent standards and monitor for negative thought pollution. We will not only be doing ourselves a great service; we will be doing others a service as well.

But this inner atmosphere is not itself negative. Like the air we breathe, it nourishes life. The positive forces of consciousness – love, compassion, forgiveness, the yearning to be reunited with the divine ground of existence – spring from those depths as well, as do the laws that express the unity of life.

In this view, the mind is as much a part of the world as matter is, and moral laws describe forces as real as those defined by laws of the physical world. Sir Isaac Newton did not invent the law of gravity; it had been floating around since creation, we might say, waiting for someone to get onto the right wavelength to pick it up. It was always there, fully operative, yet thousands of innocent souls must have been hit on the head by overripe apples over the course of history before the connection was made. It took Newton's genius and the confluence of the currents of history to allow him to delve deep into the structure of life, discern this law, and see how to apply it.

Similarly, Einstein delved into those same depths. With the wider view that Newton had opened, he was able to see gravitation as part of a larger whole and glimpse a unity in which all physical laws cohere. The relationships he found – the unity – had always been there; yet it took intense concentration, imagination, and insight to see form there, express it in laws, and work out the applications. As modern physics tells us, this is a participatory universe, whose laws are expressed in forms shaped in part by the human mind.

Spiritual laws and forces, the mystics remind us, are just as verifiable as those the physicists find. When Mahatma Gandhi said that nonviolence is the law of our being, and that it is no new discovery but "as old as the hills," he was speaking as precisely as Newton might have about gravitation. The law of life's unity is written into the very essence of creation. It comes into play whenever a person draws on the power of love and self-sacrifice to heal a relationship or stanch the spread of violence.

Yet evolution takes a great step forward when people like Gandhi, Newton, and Einstein discover such laws and articulate them in a new way, applying them scientifically to the solution of old problems. Einstein once said that even as a child, he used to imagine what the universe would look like if one could ride on a ray of light. Imagine! Most children dream of nothing more fantastical than riding on a Harley-Davidson, and here is young Albert, traveling with his imagination along sunbeams. Similarly, I like to think of Gandhi catching a ride on the force of divine love, riding it from its source deep in consciousness up to the surface of life, to show the world the way out of violence and war.

From the law of gravitation, is it too long a jump to talk about the law of love floating around in the atmosphere of our common consciousness? All we have to do is tune in and pick it up. Hate, too, is there, blowing through like a Texas tornado – don't pick it up! There is no need to bring in God or an afterlife; we all know how hatred destroys relationships between persons and races and nations. Whatever our intentions, hate gradually pollutes the atmosphere until violence erupts.

There is no use in saying to ourselves, "It can't happen here in good old Sioux Falls!" In our own century, hatred has hijacked some of the most cultured of societies. In parts of our own country, it is happening today. Unless we make a relentless, continuous effort not to open the door to hatred, we can find ourselves dwelling inside a mind that views the world with eyes of suspicion and hostility. Then we will swear that suspicion is only realistic and sympathy an attitude for fools.

"Judge not," Jesus warns, "that ye be not judged." When we keep pointing a finger of judgment at others, we are teaching our mind a lasting habit of condemnation. Sooner or later, that finger of judgment will be aimed point-blank at ourselves. It is not that people do not sometimes warrant judgment; fault is very easy to find. But judgmental attitudes and a suspicious eye only poison a situation. To right wrongs and help others correct their faults, we have to focus on what is positive and never give in to negative thinking. Love, sympathy, and forbearance require steady strength of mind.

Love means that whenever negative thoughts enter the mind, we can turn our attention to positive thoughts instead. This is all that is required to guard ourselves against lapses from love.

The key to this is giving – our time, our talents, our resources, our skills, our lives – to selfless work, some cause greater than our small personal interests. By working hard to give what we can, and by cultivating kindness and compassion under every provocation, we can escape destructive ways of thinking. Even those facing a critical illness will find that this simple prescription can lift the burdens of resentment, guilt, and depression from their lives.

When this skill of love becomes second nature, even when someone is cruel to us, our eyes will not be diverted from the divine core of his personality.

This does not mean playing Pollyanna or closing our eyes to wrong behavior. It means simply that we will never lose faith in any person's capacity to change. Without that faith, people lose faith in themselves, and without faith in yourself it is not possible to improve. Everyone deserves our respect, for all are children of an all-compassionate God. This is the most effective way to help others remember their true character.

When negative thinking ceases completely, what remains is our real nature: love itself, universal; "love without an object," as Saint Bernard says, which sheds light wherever it turns without ever asking who "deserves" it. What a question for love to ask! "I need no reason to love," Bernard says: "I love because I love; I love in order that I may love." When we attain this state we will bask in love continuously, whatever storms may rage outside. Can you imagine any greater joy? No achievement can surpass this; no aspiration can reach higher. This exalted state is our real human legacy, and until we claim it, we have not done what we are here on earth to do.

Early in this century, Werner Heisenberg changed our thinking about the world outside us by asserting that the act of observing subatomic events cannot help affecting what is observed. Mystics are no less revolutionary than quantum physicists, and what they have to tell us can lead to a transformation in our lives. "We behold that which we are, and we are that which we behold." Those who have not learned to love see a world where love is weak, ineffectual, sentimental, hopelessly out of date. Those who live in love see a world of hope: a world of men and women who, despite their failings, are always capable of love in the core of goodness in their hearts.

"He that loveth," says Thomas a Kempis, "flyeth, runneth, and rejoiceth. He is free, and will not be held in." When your love does not depend on others, you soar like an eagle, high above the selfishness of the world and its law of "an eye for an eye," which, as Mahatma Gandhi pointed out, ends only when all are blind.

To see life from this lofty vantage, however, we cannot let our sight be clouded by rumors or slander or innuendo. As long as our loyalty is dependent on other people's responses, we are living in slavery; the hallmark of love is freedom. Love "manuals" are coming out now almost like pulp novels, and their popularity reminds us how urgent is the need to rediscover what love really means. The mystics give us an uncompromisingly reliable standard: love should not waver, whatever those we love may do or say.

To lay claim to love, the mystics warn, we have to develop a fortitude that no battle in history has demanded. We have to train our mind to be secure in the teeth of deprecation, calumny, injustice, and betrayal. Only in this kind of trial by fire can the human being rise above praise and censure to that unshakable compassion which, as Jesus himself showed, is the most heroic feature of the spiritual life.

In my own lifetime, I recall how often slander was spread against Gandhi, painting him in the most lurid colors imaginable. I don't think he ever wasted a word defending himself, although it must have hurt deeply when those who should have known him better believed what they read in the more sensational papers. Even when once-loyal supporters turned against him, Gandhi's compassion for them never faltered.

Saint Francis of Assisi, who endured many similar experiences, left us his secret: "He who has not learned to forgive has lost the greatest joy in life." Every one of us has opportunities to taste this joy on a smaller scale when friends or loved ones turn against us or let us down. That is when we can transform our human love into love divine.

On the Blue Mountain in South India, where I lived for many years, sandalwood trees grow in profusion. Beautiful images of the Lord are carved from the wood of these trees, which has a lustrous texture and such a haunting fragrance that sandalwood paste is used in temple worship. If you take an axe and cut into the sandalwood tree, rich perfume comes forth; the deeper you cut, the more intoxicating the fragrance will be.

All of us, Jesus would say, can learn the lesson of forgiveness the sandalwood teaches. The deeper we are wounded, the sweeter should be our response; that is the only way to heal our wound and also to change that person's heart.

If we cannot cultivate this kind of patience, we need not bother to say we love; time will prove otherwise. We should simply use the word "like." The law of liking is: Like me and I will like you; dislike me and I will dislike you. Love is not a business contract or a trade agreement; love is a given.

Those whose responses always spring from love, in Meister Eckhart's phrase, "carry God with them in all things." That kind of love is divine. The true lover knows it is the nature of most people to change their loyalties, to modify their affections in rhythm with the ebb and flow of personal desires – and still the true lover will love.

These are marvelous challenges. It is when you begin thinking "How much will I get out of this person?" that relationships become a burden. When you are concerned only with how to give more, you feel no burden at all. Which one of us is free of self-centered thinking, even in our most intimate relationships? It may take the form of "Is she always going to be faithful?" or "Is he always going to cater to me?" Whenever we start making demands like these, at that moment the relationship turns from love.

According to the mystics, love "attempts what is above its strength." But it is just as true that love brings a surge of strength for overreaching its own limitations. When you free yourself from the conditioning of stimulus and response, so that not a ray of energy is wasted on the broken record that repeats, "What is he going to think of me," immense personal resources are released for giving. Nothing is too much for a lover to attempt, because the resources for loving have no limit. Where once we found it impossible to work with certain people, now it becomes not only possible but desirable. Those people are so hard to work with that they need somebody with patience. Seen through the eyes of love, the most difficult conditions become opportunities for helping those whom others shun. That is how the miracle of love works.

We can learn to extend our love wider and wider; without exaggeration, there is no limit to its extent. Even if for the present we can love only one person – and then only when the circumstances are just right – by daring to face difficult situations with understanding and good will, we can learn to love even people who dislike us. To me, nothing is more miraculous.

When I first came to this country in the late fifties, I was puzzled to see huge beams of light sweeping the horizon at night. I thought it must be some strange meteorological phenomenon like the aurora borealis. A friend corrected me: it was searchlights, advertising an after-hours sale on used cars. Similarly, when meditation and the Holy Name have erased selfish desire from your mind, a kind of searchlight sweeps consciousness continuously, bathing it in light. This quiet inner light marks the presence of the man or woman who has achieved life's highest goal: not only to love Jane and Chuck and little Betsy, but to love everyone on earth, without exception.

As our desire to draw closer to the Lord within us deepens, it draws self-centered desires into it like tributaries into a great river. The power of that love swells until it becomes cataclysmic; we begin to inspire other people through the transformation we have wrought in ourselves. They say to themselves, "I knew him when he was nothing but trouble, and now look at him! There is hope even for me." In this way, we quietly begin to be a force for good.

The Lord is love itself. Christ asks us to endure persecution "on my account," and his account has no limits. We can write checks on it anytime we need to, anywhere we happen to be, and there will always be resources to cover the draft. The more we get ourselves out of the way, the easier will be our access to this limitless treasury of love in the depths of the heart.

When our relationships become strained, we can ask ourselves what Jesus would have done – or, when that seems too lofty, what Saint Teresa or Saint Francis would have done. The example of such figures shows with what thoroughness divine love can transform ordinary men and women, who began with all the human frailties we recognize in ourselves. They show us that if we want to learn to love, we have to rise above low and demeaning responses – little by little, day by day, situation by situation. It is not at all easy; it has never been easy for anybody. Yet nothing is more rewarding.

The Lord is in everyone; therefore we must practice love and trust and selfless service with everyone every-

where. Whenever you look into another person's eyes, remember that you are looking into a city where the Lord
dwells – and remember always that our arms and hands
were given to us for others' rescue, not for their ruin.

We come from God and dwell in God, the mystics say,
and to God we shall return. This supreme Being, whom
galaxies cannot contain, lives in the small confines of
every human heart. Whenever I hear what a miracle the
artificial heart is, I remind myself that the greatest miracle
is that the Lord is enshrined in the heart of the soul.
Whatever we may do, he never gives up and moves away;
he is always there. We should learn to give every person
the same kind of respect, and never give up on anybody.
When we can do this, we will live in joy always. Even
tragedy cannot drive this joy away, because it comes not
from what life gives us but from our boundless capacity to
give.

Love of this power and sweep has very practical consequences. Tensions are released, conflicts resolved; vitality, enthusiasm, creativity, and resourcefulness are re-
newed for us every day. Every human faculty, in fact,
comes to function beautifully. The reason is simple: we
are no longer squandering and fractioning our energy on
ourselves. All our vitality is merged in one mighty force
which we offer to life as a great gift, and life itself repays us
abundantly. This is the wonderful reward that divine love
brings.

★

Finally, we are getting to the bottom of love's mysteries.
We are no longer confusing love with the urge to be intimate with two or three people who satisfy our emotional
needs; we are talking about catching a ride on a force
powerful enough to make our trouble-plagued world a
paradise. It takes years of practice, but the same mental
power we expend every day in keeping private desires

burning can slowly be harnessed in bringing people together, in healing relationships, in resolving some of the
long-standing difficulties that stand between us and a
world at peace.

The regular practice of meditation and repetition of the
mantram can be compared to building a road deep into the
unconscious, where the forces of love and hatred play.
Ask your grandparents how much engineering effort went
into building some of the highways in this country. Rivers
had to be spanned, slopes graded, mountains tunneled
through. The road into deeper consciousness requires
every bit as much skill and painstaking attention. The
challenges – and the dangers, I might as well say – are
practically unending. But the reward is access to a realm
where personalities and events can be seen as fluid energy,
waiting to be shaped by the power of love.

It is only when we live on the surface of life, driven
about by personal urges, that little things can satisfy us or
upset us. As we sink below the surface, we begin to feel
the draw of a current of irresistible love, carrying us
toward the very depths of consciousness. There is no "I"
or "you" in these deep realms; there is only all. The self-
naughting which is such a recurring theme in the literature
of mysticism is simply preparation for being admitted to
this divine condition. The camel trying to squeeze
through the eye of a needle is a lively illustration of how
little selfhood we must have in order to get in.

Yet paradoxically, it is only here, where the sense of a
separate personality is zero, that all our human needs are
met. As the very nature of God implies, our needs are infinite. The Lord is our very Self, and nothing less than his
infinitude can satisfy us. "How could I find rest anywhere
else," asks Augustine, "when I was made to find my rest
in thee?" This is not metaphysics; it is the plain dynamics
of love. Our need is for a state of unity that will never
leave us; nothing less will do. Only in the depths of the

soul, beyond time, place, change, and circumstance, can we find the fulfillment of our deep need to love.

Even in the midst of turmoil and trouble, those who have learned to turn their back on personal grievances and return kindness for unkindness live in heaven on earth. No external event can shake the security this love brings. Those who possess it may live in the midst of Manhattan or in the suburbs of Sacramento; they still live every day in the kingdom of heaven. That is their permanent state. They don't have to try to love; they cannot help it, and everyone who comes within their orbit will be touched by their lives.

Laboring under conditions we would find too primitive to believe, with the handicap of superiors who put up obstacles to her work, Saint Teresa of Avila carried her love throughout Spain; ultimately it spread around the world. The king of Spain at that time was an inordinately powerful and wealthy man; yet was he able to have that kind of influence over history? All the crowned heads of Europe together had not one percent of Teresa's impact. Burning love enabled her to do the impossible: to reach deep into the hearts of people everywhere and stir them to change their lives.

Teresa was not a bit shy about giving away her secret: *Amor saca amor,* "Love begets love." Even if you try to resist love of this magnitude, she says, it reaches out like a sword and opens up your heart to draw love out of you.

When Gandhi came back to India from South Africa in 1915, a stranger in his own country, who would have dreamed that he would bring the British Empire to its knees? Yet it was not Gandhi who brought it down, as he would have been the first to admit. It was the power of love, working through the hearts of millions of responsive people in India, in Great Britain, and elsewhere around the world.

Whatever their differences in language and life-style,

great lovers like Teresa and Gandhi saw the Lord in the heart of every person around them. This is the vision that enabled them to treat others with love and respect even in the heat of opposition. It may take time, but no one is immune to this kind of love; it draws a response from everyone.

For men and women with this kind of vision, love becomes a passion that will not let them rest. No matter what comes in the way, they are going to carry forward that work. Physically, of course, there comes a time when they disappear from this earth, just as Teresa and Gandhi have. But their work continues. Their lives continue, working through those they inspire.

Mystics would say that the spirit of someone like Teresa of Avila is abroad, looking for ordinary human beings like us to pick up. We read her life and words and they stir something deep inside us, moving us to take up spiritual disciplines and make changes that seemed impossible before. In this way, with our wholehearted consent, divine love can take possession of our life and gradually make it an instrument of peace on earth.

More than one lover of God has called him the hunter of souls. Here is Teresa:

> When that tender hunter from paradise
> Released his piercing arrow at me,
> My wounded soul fell in his loving arms,
> And my life is so completely transformed
> That my Beloved One has become mine
> And without a doubt I am his at last.

Teresa of Avila wrote a number of exquisite love poems like this about the one she called "His Majesty," who hunted her down with inescapable grace and shot her separate self out from under her. After that shot she could well have said, like Paul, "I died, and yet I live: yet not I, but Christ liveth in me."

Every human being finds this painful. Yet if the day

comes that it happens to us, we too will sing our joy; for after this wound we can no longer behave selfishly. We are bonded by compassion to all who suffer. We can forgive them their lapses because we recall only too clearly what the affliction of self-centeredness is like; and we can help them because our hearts are free to give.

Only then, when we have given up once and for all the frantic effort to shape the world around ourselves, do other people trust us completely. Until that time we cannot guess what being loved and cherished really is. We have a saying in India: "When the lotus blooms, it doesn't have to go looking for bees." Bees are always bumbling around in search of flowers; that is their job. Similarly, we human beings are all searching for love. Those who have learned to give compassion freely, asking nothing as collateral, have no need to take out an ad in the classified section: "Love Available. Call 694-LOVE." We seek out such people and are drawn to them; we just can't help ourselves.

Lest we doubt the joy of it, here is the testimony of the English mystic Richard Rolle, as true and as eccentric a troubador of God as Saint Francis was, and one of the earliest poets of the English language. Read it aloud and listen to the way it sings of joy:

> Song I call, when in a plenteous soul the sweetness of eternal love with burning is taken, and thought into song is turned, and the mind into full sweet sound is changed.
> . . . O singular joy of love everlasting, that ravishes all His to heavens above all worlds, them binding with bands of virtue! O dear charity, in earth that has thee not is nought wrought, whatever it hath! He truly that in thee is busy, to joy above earthly is soon lifted!
> Thou makest men contemplative, heaven-gate thou openest, mouths of accusers thou dost shut, God thou makest to be seen and multitude of sins thou hidest. We praise thee, we preach thee, by thee

the world we quickly overcome, by whom we joy and the heavenly ladder we ascend.

And again Rolle tells what transformations this love works in the souls of those it seizes:

But this grace generally and to all is not given, but to the holy soul imbued with the holiest is taught; in whom the excellence of love shines, and songs of lovely loving, Christ inspiring, commonly burst up, and being made as it were a pipe of love, joying sounds.

The which [soul] the mystery of love knowing, with great cry to its Love ascends, in wit sharpest, and in knowledge and in feeling subtle; not spread in things of this world but into God all gathered and set, that in cleanness of conscience and shining of soul to Him it may serve whom it has purposed to love, and itself to Him to give.

Surely the clearer the love of the lover is, the nearer to him and the more present God is. And thereby more clearly in God he joys, and of the sweet Goodness the more he feels, that to lovers is wont Itself to inshed, and to mirth without comparison the hearts of the meek to turn.

The triumphant, joyful note of freedom in those lines is the sure mark of the mystic. Above all else, the lover of God is free, because freedom is the breath and soul of love. "As long as you stand hat in hand begging life for favors," my spiritual teacher used to tell me, "life will have only contempt for you." When people get anxious and insecure, allowing themselves to become upset over every little thing, it is essentially because of this attitude: they are forever asking life for favors. And Granny would add: "Don't make demands on life that life cannot fulfill."

It took decades of frustration for me to understand those words, but today I don't make any demands on life at all. All I need is opportunities for giving, which life has no power to withhold.

Not long ago I was leaving San Francisco with some

friends at the end of a gorgeous day. Commuters were streaming into the main arteries of the city, and as we turned onto Van Ness Avenue and headed north I thought to myself that it would take half an hour just to reach the Golden Gate Bridge. Ahead of us a long row of forbidding red lights warned me to settle back and repeat my mantram. But as we drove, miraculously enough, light after light turned green. The friend who was driving me timed it perfectly; we never so much as slowed down until we saw the red towers of the bridge poking overhead into the mist.

That is how our lives can be. With this one commitment to live for all, your personal life becomes smooth sailing. Minor problems which used to mean gridlock will break up and get out of your way.

Then a new joy enters your life. Most of us, I imagine, truly believe that just doing our thing, doing what we want, is the height of a good day. But the joy of loving and serving others is a million times greater. Once we get even a taste of this joy, we will not be able to restrain ourselves from giving and loving more.

Isn't being in love the highest joy we know? Romance must sell more books, more movie tickets, more concert seats, than all other subjects combined. Now imagine for a moment how much joy there must be in love that can never fail, that never ends or wavers or runs dry. Imagine the joy of never losing faith in someone we love, in loving him just as intensely no matter what he does. We would get to keep the joy of our love and never lose it. Then try to imagine feeling that kind of continuous, unconditional love not just for one person but for all. That is the joy these mystics have found.

If we live selfishly, not all the angels in the celestial spheres will be able to drag us into heaven. But if we love all life, all people, all creatures, we have found heaven already; we live in heaven here on earth. The choice is ours, and it is within our reach, as the medieval monk Fra Giovanni testifies in words that are perfect for meditation:

> There is nothing I can give you which you do not have, but there is much that while I cannot give it, you can take. No heaven can come to us unless our hearts find rest in today. Take heaven. No peace lies in the future which is not hidden in this present instant. Take peace.
>
> The gloom of the world is but a shadow behind it, yet within reach is joy. There is radiance and glory in the darkness could we but see, and to see we have only to look. I beseech you to look.
>
> Life is so generous a giver, but we, judging its gifts by their covering, cast them away as ugly or hard; remove the covering and you will find beneath it a living splendor, woven of love, by wisdom, with power.
>
> Welcome it, grasp it, and you touch the angel's hand that brings it to you. Everything we call a trial, a sorrow or a duty, the angel's hand is there, the gift is there and the wonder of an overshadowing presence. Our joys too, be not content with them as joys. They too conceal diviner gifts.
>
> And so at this time I greet you, not quite as the world sends greetings but with profound esteem and the prayer that for you, now and forever, the day breaks and the shadows flee away.

Mercy

*Blessed are the merciful, for they shall obtain
mercy.*

"THE POSSESSION OF GOD," says Ruysbroeck,
"demands and supposes active love. He who thinks or
feels otherwise is deceived." To be full of love, full to
overflowing, so full that we give love freely to everyone
around us – in the end, the mystics ask, isn't this what we
all want in life, more than anything else? This full measure
of love has a healing effect not only on those around us,
but also on ourselves.

The whole message of original goodness is that we do
not have to work to draw this kind of love from some external source. A full reservoir of love is lying right inside
us. In meditation we are digging deep into our own consciousness, tunneling toward this infinite reservoir that
lies waiting to be discovered and manifested in our daily
life.

"Come unto me," Jesus promises, "all ye that labor and
are heavy laden, and I will give you rest. Take my yoke

upon you, and learn of me, for I am meek and lowly in heart: and ye shall find rest unto your souls." When we are kind, tender, compassionate, and forgiving, we get a glimpse of the healing power of this reservoir of mercy within.

But I do not want to soften this statement from the Beatitudes: "Blessed are the merciful, for they shall obtain mercy." If we listen to it with our hearts, we will hear a thunderclap. Who will obtain the mercy we all long for from life? Only the loving, only those who show mercy to others. Only those who forgive others will enjoy the healing power of forgiveness in themselves, because in showing mercy to others we are being merciful with ourselves as well.

The reason is simple: only then are we abiding by life's most fundamental law, that all of us are one. If I give love to others, it means, I stand to benefit from that love as much as they. Not necessarily immediately, not necessarily directly, but that love has to come back to me; for I have added to the measure of love in the world, the mystics say, and I am part of that whole. Similarly, if I add meanness, stinginess, resentment, hostility, then sooner or later that sort of treatment will be shown to me.

This is not so occult as it may sound. After all, when someone treats us unkindly, isn't it natural that we begin to avoid that person, speak curtly, even be unkind ourselves? When a person is regularly unkind, it conditions our expectations; then, when that person surprises us with something thoughtful – it *does* happen! – we may shun him anyway, simply out of habit. It is the same with kindness: when we can count on a person to be loving, we give our love freely in return, and allow a wide margin for those rare times when he or she might act otherwise. "She's never like that," we tell ourselves. "Something terrible must be preying on her mind." That is how our responses to life come back to us.

In Hindu and Buddhist mysticism, this commonsense principle is called the law of karma. The word *karma* has been much misunderstood, but its literal meaning is simply action, something done. So instead of using exotic language, we might as well refer to the "law of action," which states that everything we do – even everything we think, since our thoughts condition our behavior – has consequences: not "equal and opposite" as in physics, but equal and alike. The comparison with physics is deliberate, for this is not a doctrine of any particular religion. It is a law of life, which no one has stated more clearly than Jesus: "Judge not, that ye be not judged. For with what judgment ye judge, ye shall be judged: and with what measure ye mete, it shall be meted unto you." Paul puts it more tersely: "As we sow, so shall we reap." The working of this law is not necessarily negative, as this Beatitude shows: if we sow mercy, we shall receive it in ample harvest.

Even if we follow these arguments intellectually, however, how many of us act as if this law really applied to us? We let mercy wait while we pursue goals we understand. A luxurious home overlooking the sea through a forest of pines; prestige in our job, success for our children: don't all of us dream that such things can make us happy? We slave for them. "That is not enough," Jesus would say quietly. Our need is for love, and we can get it only in the measure that we give.

Instead of pursuing external satisfactions, Jesus tells us, we need to let mercy rule our decisions from day to day, and our long-range goals as well. Then the forces of life will rise up from within to protect us. They will protect our health by keeping us clear of physical addictions and emotional obsessions. They will protect our mind by keeping it calm and detached. People will surround us with affection and support when they see we care about them more than we do about ourselves. And as death approaches, it will hold no fear for us. We will know for certain that the forces of mercy from which we draw our life flow through creation from an endless source, and will never cease flowing.

Just as our currency was once guaranteed by gold reserves, every word Jesus delivers in the Beatitudes is guaranteed by his life. How many times Jesus forgave in the face of cruelty! It is the example of his life that gives his words on forgiveness the power to penetrate our hearts even after two thousand years.

Even on the scale of international politics, when some minister of state proclaims, "We have been provoked and our only course is retaliation," Jesus' reminder of mercy should echo in our ears. What a challenge he is issuing us! But if forgiveness is truly a law of life, then retaliating only makes others more angry, less open to discussion, and more vengeful than before. If we will only put forward a helping hand, Jesus is urging us – even before we are asked – the laws that govern human nature above and beyond political persuasion or race or religion will eventually stir a deeply human response, which can defuse the most desperate of situations. Later I will let Mahatma Gandhi tell us of his experiences putting mercy to work on large-scale social problems. His experience is an abiding affirmation that practicing this Beatitude can bring about no less than the end of war and the beginning of real peace, which this world has scarcely known.

"Be kind, be kind, be kind." That is the prescription for holiness issued by a wise medieval mystic. Half its wisdom lies in its insistence on being kind over and over; for to make kindness the mind's natural response even in the unconscious requires years of practice. Until we descend into the depths of the mind, we simply have no idea what resentments have accumulated there. "In these regions," says the theologian Paul Tillich, we can find hidden hostilities against those with whom we are in love. We can find envy and torturing doubt about whether we are really accepted by them. And this hostility and anxiety about being rejected by those who are nearest us can hide itself under the various forms of love: friendship, sensual love, conjugal and family love.

Even today, in this age of practical psychology, people are so insecure that without realizing it, they often try to raise themselves up by tearing somebody else down. When we get even a glimpse of the unity of life, we realize that in tearing others down we are tearing ourselves down too. Sitting in judgment on other people and countries and races is training your mind to sit in judgment on yourself. "Forgive us our trespasses, as we forgive those who trespass against us." As we forgive others, we are teaching the mind to respond with forgiveness everywhere, even to the misdeeds and mistakes of our own past.

Yet true forgiveness is no simple matter of shaking hands and murmuring, "Forget it, old boy." Careful files are being kept inside. Little grievances, injuries that don't deserve a second thought, are being recorded deep in consciousness, marked "Store Indefinitely. Top Secret." These are the episodes that come up in dreams, cause us conflicts, and often push us to erupt in unexpected bouts of temper. In very deep meditation you will actually catch sight of some of these hang-ups. And you gasp: that grudge you have been feeding all these years has been responsible for emotional sore spots and health problems you never suspected.

Indulging in anger is pointing a poison-tipped arrow inward, aimed straight at ourselves. It taints our thinking, poisons our feelings, turns our relationships adversarial. If we continue to think resentful thoughts, mistrust spreads in consciousness like some toxic underground chemical until we have a permanent disposition for suspicion. When anger pollutes our internal environment to this extent, we don't need particular events to trigger suspicion; it has become an automatic response, draining us of energy like an insidious hidden leak. Our nervous system and vital organs react angrily on their own, without any connivance from the mind. The long-term effects, as I said earlier, can be disastrous: heart disease, stroke, extreme emotional stress, perhaps even lower resistance to disease and impaired capacity to heal.

★

To counter this tendency of the mind, we need some way to gain access to the deep reservoir of mercy within. But how? This is a question that will touch every choice we make, because part of the answer is that we must learn to harness and use wisely the energies of our lives.

Energy conservation is the basis of spiritual engineering, for vital energy provides the power we need to tap the infinite source of goodness and mercy that lies at the core of consciousness.

In Sanskrit, vital energy is called *prana,* which literally means "the energy of life." Prana is the energy that drives the whole organism we call ourself: not only the physical body, but the mind as well. All creatures consume vital energy. In the ancient Hindu tradition, it is said that we come into life with a given supply of this energy, enough to power a certain number of breathing cycles. Our natural human life span, according to this view, is allotted not in calendar years but in the number of breaths we take. The word *expire* means literally to reach the end of this span of breaths – interestingly enough, at about one hundred and twenty years of age. Anything less is considered a premature death, "death by unnatural causes."

If this theory is true, it may help to explain why these ancient sages claim a close connection between mental states and longevity. Our breathing rhythm, the measure of how fast our reserves of vital energy are being consumed, is regulated in part by our state of mind. Security, compassion, patience, forgiveness – all these are accompanied, if you observe closely, by a relatively slow breathing rhythm and heart rate. Positive states of mind like these conserve energy and lengthen the life span, leaving a reserve of resilience and resistance for facing challenges. Every time we are able to remain calm under pressure, or merciful while under attack, we are making a big deposit into the vault of vital energy within.

Learning to control attention is the key to gaining access to this energy and using it wisely. No skill in living is more useful. It is William James again who writes that the ability to direct attention "is the very root of judgment, character and will." Human attention is the equivalent of a turbocharged sports car with space-age aerodynamics: we can use its power to take us wherever we want. We can turn corners with a flick of the wrist, brake fast if necessary to avoid an accident; we can even turn the ignition off when the engine needs a rest. "An education which should include this faculty," James continues, "would be the education *par excellence*." Sadly, I know of no curriculum in any educational system in the world for learning this most basic of skills.

When you can keep your attention where you want it, vital wealth accumulates, like savings earning compound interest. You become so loaded with cash reserves that it becomes very difficult to upset you. When J. Paul Getty lost five dollars, do you think he called in the police? Even five hundred would scarcely have been noticed. Mastering attention can make you that kind of tycoon with your vitality; you can take great losses without ever losing your balance.

Yet most of us live from hand to mouth, writing energy checks every time we think life has let us down. What a way to go through life, squandering our vital wealth just to keep ourselves in emotional poverty! Our piggy bank never gets full enough to make a deposit, so if somebody grabs a nickel from us, naturally we cannot sleep.

All of us need ways to conserve and replenish our emotional reserves. What meditation can do over a period of many years is open up access to a limitless supply of vital wealth. After all these decades I still meditate for hours every day, just as an oil tycoon drills for oil and natural gas, to tap greater and greater resources for carrying on this work. The miracle is that once you reach this stage, maintaining complete and uninterrupted attention no longer requires effort. Full attention, and therefore full vitality, becomes your natural state.

When somebody is talking to me, for example – even one of the children in the midst of a conversation among adults – I never fail to give my complete attention, no matter what else is going on around us. "Quality attention," some psychologists call it. The natural tendency of the mind is to wander, but I have taught it to focus and stay still. After years of practice it cannot behave in any other way. The bonus is priceless: intimate, unbreakable relationships.

One benefit of this kind of control over attention is the capacity for unshakable loyalty. I never give up on anybody, and I am not exaggerating in the least when I tell you that no joy in life is more exhilarating. When Saint Francis insists that it is in loving that we are loved, this is what he means. When your love for others cannot be shaken by anything they do, you never ask whether they love you; it is irrelevant. That is what unconditional love means, and naturally it draws a loving response.

Young people, to me, are the real wealth of any country. That is no mere cliché; it is a living truth. And the best way to help our young people discover and harness their inner resources is by teaching them to master their attention, beginning with our own example. Giving children our full attention is the best way to make them secure; and with the steadiness that comes from a trained mind, we will not lose faith when they run into the problems that young people run into everywhere. Our support will give them a safety net while they are learning to deal with life, which today is an unparalleled challenge for anyone. With that net, even if they fall, they are much less likely to get hurt.

Attention is trained not only during meditation but throughout the day, by keeping your attention off yourself and focused on the job at hand. Going through the day with a one-pointed mind is itself quite an achievement. But after many years of effort, imperceptibly, a tiny hole opens in consciousness. You will have to work for a long time, like a woodpecker, to open that hole further. Years of peck-peck-pecking away lie ahead. But when the opening is wide enough, you can shine your attention like a powerful flashlight into deeper realms of consciousness.

This is an extraordinary experience, for which nothing in the external world can prepare us. Everywhere you look you see the forces of consciousness at play, surging through the shadow-world of the mind. There is anger, barreling through like a freight train; don't get in its way! And there is desire, rising nebulous from the deep. The marvelous thing about watching these forces is that without even realizing it, you begin to understand that they have no intrinsic power to compel your actions. You are not linked inextricably to the thoughts these forces conjure up: in fact, you are not your mind at all.

As your concentration deepens, the beam of its searchlight penetrates farther and farther into the gloom. It is the power of harnessed passions which gives that light such enormous penetrating power. Slowly, unconscious forces are coming under the control of your conscious mind.

Meditation is the drill we use day by day to widen that opening. Ultimately it enables us to reach deep into the unconscious, almost to the seabed of consciousness, and draw these clamoring forces into one irresistible surge of love. "This abyss of wisdom," says Saint John of the Cross, "now lifts up and enlarges the soul, giving it to drink at the very sources of the science of love."

★

This reservoir of energy in the depths of consciousness is available to all human beings, but access is far from easy. Like an exclusive country club surrounded by unscalable walls, the vaults of the unconscious are jealously guarded. There is only one way to get hold of the Gold Card that allows uninhibited admission: we have to live entirely for the benefit of all. Only then will the Lord allow us past the gate.

For this, mastery of attention alone is not enough. With concentration must flow what in traditional religious language is called devotion: love of God. We already have the capacity for devotion, the mystics say, even if we don't know it. The problem is that it is locked up in any number of personal attachments: to our home, our job, our clothes; even in compulsive attachments to family and friends. Let me emphasize again, this is quite different from loving God in all; here the emphasis is on *our* needs and wants.

Most of us carry strong personal attachments and sincerely believe that we love deeply. But when we are emotionally entangled with someone, we cannot really be aware of that person's needs or how we affect his life. Our preoccupation is with ourselves: that our feelings not be violated and that our wants be fulfilled. One frank Christian mystic goes so far as to describe attachment as "mercenary love." We say, "I will love Clothilde so long as she does A, B, and C and never dreams of doing X, Y, and Z." This is more akin to a business contract than to love. Love means always taking into consideration how our words and actions might affect those around us. This is how we make our love more pure.

A compulsive attachment is trapped energy, and its pressure builds up tremendously over time. We have difficulty pulling our attention away from the other person and devoting this energy to the kind of lofty goal that alone can give life meaning. Conversely, real love opens up the very wellsprings of vitality for selfless service. When we learn to love truly, selflessly, all the power that had been trapped in private, personal attachments comes gushing up into our lives.

All this ties in closely with self-indulgence. Every time we yield to a personal desire, there is some satisfaction, of course, but we have also written a check on our vital energy account. After we have been dashing off checks right and left for some time, depression often sets in. We feel so drained that we just can't cope with the rigors of the day. This low-energy ebb is the manager of the bank inside reminding us, "Don't write so many checks. They're starting to bounce!"

This happens whenever the mind gets excited, and the more agitation there is in the mind, the more energy is lost. My submission is that the exhilaration from certain potent drugs and from sexual stimulation makes a particularly large draw on our energy reserves. Since not only the heart and lungs but all physiological systems – including the immune system – draw on this energy for proper functioning, anything that depletes energy reserves regularly is likely to take a toll on health. Compulsive self-indulgence is always debilitating, and over time it may well lower our resistance to disease.

I took some young friends to a frozen yogurt shop the other day, and while they were deciding between White Chocolate–Macadamia and Very Raspberry, a hand-printed sign on the counter caught my eye: "Now is not the time for self-restraint." It gave me pause. How little we understand the vital connection between self-restraint and love! Excessive indulgence actually drains our power to love, blocks our vision of others' needs. Our senses and passions are always on their feet, waving their arms in our face and exclaiming, "Hey, you, I want this! Look over there, how can you resist that!" With all this hullabaloo, it takes effort even to notice that other people are around.

It always surprises listeners when I say that people who have a strong sex drive should congratulate themselves. They have a lot of gas in their tank, a lot of vital energy in reserve. But gas is to be used, not drained; if you let your car sit with a hole in the tank, you are likely to be out of fuel when you need it most. The stronger a person's sexual desires, the more vital it is that the power behind these desires be harnessed. What I never hesitate to deprecate is adults continuing to maintain teenage attitudes about sex long after they have passed the age of discretion. And it is not only behavior that drains vitality. Reading about it, seeing stimulating movies, fantasizing – all these consume large amounts of prana.

Behind sexual desire is a very natural longing that is not really physical: the longing to escape the loneliness of separate existence. The closer we learn to feel to other people, the less we will be driven by the physical urge for sex, for the urge will be fulfilled much closer to its source. As we deepen our relationships far below the physical level, the sexual drive will be transformed naturally into a dynamo of creative power: the power to help, the power to love.

★

Several years ago my wife and I visited a retreat in the Southwest, where I was to speak on meditation. It was my first visit to that part of the country, and I found the scenery spectacular in its beauty.

One day our hosts took us to see a stunning chapel built

up against the red sandstone of the desert hills. As we entered, I felt as if I had received a blow. Right in front of us rose a lifelike sculpture of Christ in agony on the cross. The eyes were hollow with pain and the mouth seemed to be crying out, "Haven't I suffered long enough? Can't you all join hands now and lift me down from this cross?"

Whenever we utter an angry word or raise a hand against our neighbor, we are driving in another nail to keep Jesus up on that cross. The principle underlying the Passion is that out of his infinite mercy, the Lord has taken our suffering upon himself. As long as any living creature is in pain, so is Jesus, for he lives at the heart of all. Wherever violence breaks out, no matter how cleverly we try to justify it, we are crucifying the spirit of Christ.

"Patience" and "passion" both come from a Latin word meaning to suffer or endure. When we speak of the Passion of Christ, we are recalling the suffering he endured on the cross. But it is good to realize that whenever we practice patience – cheerfully bearing with somebody who is irascible, or enduring discomfort rather than imposing it on others – in a small way we are embracing the principle of the Passion. Each of us can bear a little of such self-denial, and with practice, our shoulders can grow broad enough to carry some of the burden of those we love. In this way, the mystics tell us, by practicing mercy throughout our lives, we take upon ourselves some of Jesus' burden of pain.

This does not mean becoming blind to what others are doing. That is not what mercy and forgiveness mean. I know when somebody is being rude or unkind, but it does not impair my faith in that person or lower him in my eyes. I keep my eyes on the core of goodness I see in him, and act toward him as I would have him act toward me. There is only one way to make others more loving, and that is by loving more ourselves.

What we are looking for in others is generally what we find. "Such as we are inwardly," Thomas a Kempis says, "so we judge outwardly." Psychology can go no deeper. If we want to follow Jesus' dictum to "judge not," we must change who we are; then others will change in our own eyes. When we ourselves are trustworthy, for example, we see others the same and trust them accordingly – and when we do, interestingly enough, our trust is often rewarded. Trust is a two-way street. It is the same with our other judgments about life: it's amazing how quickly the world we live in conforms itself to our ideas about it.

You can test this intriguing law in the laboratory of your own life. If someone at work absolutely seems to enjoy making things rougher for you, try treating that person with extra respect – and go on showing him respect no matter how he acts. In a surprisingly short time, I predict, his behavior will begin to verify your faith in his better side.

Yet I need hardly remind you how hard it is to start letting down old, ingrained hostile defenses. Experience, we believe, does not teach us that others are trustworthy; it teaches us that we had better watch our flanks. The memory of past letdowns can weigh down any sensitive human being, making trust an elusive commodity to acquire. Worst of all, when negative memories cast a shadow of mistrust over our relationships, we lack the vitality we need to withdraw our attention and act with kindness, as if those shadows were not there. That is why any effective reformation of character has to start with reforming the thought process itself.

Here the power of the Holy Name makes itself felt. Each time your thoughts start to wander down dark alleyways of the past, by drawing on the Holy Name you can call them back and point their feet in the direction you really want them to go. Gradually, with practice, your thoughts will wander much less frequently; in time, they may even forget the address of those alleyways they once haunted.

Repeating the Holy Name is a powerful way to harness a very natural tendency of the human mind: to brood. Every compulsion gets its grip from this tendency. The mind takes a trifling remark or incident, no bigger than a limp balloon, and starts to inflate it by thinking about it over and over and over, blowing it up with its attention until it fills our consciousness and we cannot think about anything else.

When the mind starts this blow-up routine, the Holy Name restores your perspective by letting out the air. Every time the mind pumps, the Holy Name pricks open a little hole and lets some of your attention get free. The balloon may not collapse immediately – after all, an emotion like anger or resentment has powerful lungs. But right from the first, it will not get so obsessively large, which means you have introduced a measure of free choice. Next time you will find your freedom even greater.

When, after years of sincere repetition, you make the Holy Name an integral part of your consciousness, it can take even a grievous injury and reduce it to such a minuscule size that forgiveness comes easily. Afterward, when you recall the incident, there will be no emotional charge. Then personal relationships become effortlessly comfortable. You will be able to work easily even with people who have done you a bad turn, because past memories will have no more power to compel you than would the memory of some old film.

Once at a swimming pool I saw a fascinating device that moves around the pool keeping the water clean. The Holy Name is a pool sweep for the mind, sweeping away resentment and frustration before they get a chance to build up during the day. A burden of resentment, carried around for years, translates into constant mental turmoil, which expresses itself in physical and psychosomatic ailments. A mind kept clean of resentment, whatever the provocation, not only is resourceful and secure but also makes the body less prone to physical problems.

It is not quite accurate, however, to say that anger is swept away. Another way of describing the process is that emotions like anger are transformed. Anger is power. When I see instances of injustice – which I do every day now in the newspapers and magazines – I get enormously angry. For example, coming from India, I still identify with the plight of the Third World. I grieve every time I am reminded that half a billion people, most of them children, go to bed hungry each night. I don't have to see them face to face to feel their suffering; they are right there in my consciousness. But as that anger rises, it is transformed into creative energy for selfless action. That is why you will never hear me waste a word on judging, haranguing, and complaining. My time and energy go into teaching others how to live by the unity of life, so that these wrongs can be set right. Anger is now a kind of backyard oil well, to draw on when I need power. Mahatma Gandhi was instrumental in showing us how crude anger can be transformed into refined energy to drive the engine of mercy.

The machinery for this transformation is very simple in design: we have only to cease making selfish demands on life. I don't try to clutch at people any longer, or to cling to pleasures. I don't rely on applause and appreciation for security, because I depend entirely upon the Lord within. That is why anxiety has gone out of my life; frustration has fled; every negative emotion is but a distant memory.

I have come to have an all-consuming passion for every creature on earth: for all countries, all races, all animals. My appeals to help save the elephants in Africa, in danger of extinction from poaching because of consumer demand for ivory, is a natural part of the unitive vision. It is said of Margery Kempe, an English mystic of the fourteenth century, that "if she saw a man with a wound, or a beast, or if a man beat a child before her, or smote a horse with a whip, she saw our Lord being beaten or wounded."Sri Ramakrishna, one of the greatest of India's mystics, used to feel such wounds on his own body.

Such a tremendous backlog of energy can be locked up in anger and resentment that we can visualize it as a Hoover Dam right inside, blocking our energy flow on every level from the physical to the spiritual. The most effective way I know to channel the enormous power of anger is to turn it around, turn it into mercy, by pouring it into the peaceful resolution of problems that threaten to erupt in violence between individuals and communities and nations. Working for the sake of all releases a virtual flood of creative energy into our lives.

★

In practice, mercy is just what Mahatma Gandhi meant by nonviolence. Nonviolence is much more than a technique for righting social wrongs; it is the mercy which Jesus beseeches us to practice in every arena of our life. "In my opinion nonviolence is not passive in any shape or form," Gandhi wrote. "Nonviolence, as I understand it, is the most active force in the world." He is talking about the mercy that flows from our heart when we have smashed through the dam of hatred.

I like to think of Gandhi as an energy tycoon, constantly drilling for the oil of mercy and pumping it up to allay violence, harnessing anger's fierce power in constructive action. But he is extremely practical about how we must go about this process of drilling. "If one does not practice nonviolence in one's personal relations with others and hopes to use it in bigger affairs, one is vastly mistaken. Nonviolence, like charity, must begin at home."

One man who took Gandhi at his word was Martin Luther King, Jr. When I was at the University of Minnesota as a Fulbright scholar in 1959, some of the students in my dorm came to my room one evening and said, "You're interested in Gandhi. Someone you should hear is speaking tonight. Come on." Still new to the country, I hadn't even heard about Martin Luther King, but I went and sat with them, right in front.

The auditorium filled until it was packed. Then a quiet black man stood up, walked to the podium, and began to speak. I couldn't believe my ears: he was speaking the very language of Gandhi, not quoting him but speaking with the unmistakable conviction of living, personal experience. Later I found that he had been to India to learn about Gandhi's experiments in nonviolence.

In one shining passage from a recent biography, King recalls a night in 1956 when his work, his family, his very life were threatened by the roused forces of oppression. While his wife and child slept, he sat in despair at the kitchen table with his head in his hands, about to give up the struggle. From the depths of his consciousness he prayed aloud: "Lord, I'm down here trying to do what's right. . . . But Lord, I must confess that I'm weak now. I'm faltering. I'm losing my courage."

And a voice from within uttered clearly: "Stand up for righteousness. Stand up for justice. Stand up for truth. And lo I will be with you, even until the end of the world."

In that moment, King tells us, he lost his fears of failure; he lost the very fear of death. And from that night on, his work began to bear miraculous fruit.

We may not be called to face such challenges, but wherever we have difficulty getting along with somebody, that is a precious opportunity to start drilling for mercy. "It is only when you meet with resistance," Gandhi wrote, "that your nonviolence is put on trial."

I confess to having been baffled for decades by that phrase "getting even." If you really want to get even with someone, be more forgiving; kindness exchanged for unkindness comes out even. What people call getting even is only getting odd. That wise old fellow Ben Franklin understood: "Next to knowing when to seize an opportunity," he said, "the most important thing to know in life is when to forgo an advantage."

"Mutual forbearance," wrote Gandhi, "is nonviolence. Immediately, therefore, you get the conviction that nonviolence is the law of life, you have to practice it towards those who act violently towards you, and the law must apply to nations as [to] individuals." Then he adds, "Training no doubt is necessary. And beginnings are always small."

I must tell you that even though I grew up in Gandhi's India, my own beginnings in this art were small indeed. My village in South India had no high school until I entered my teens, so of course there were quite a few older fellows in my class who had finished the lower grades years before. Some were twice my age and seemed twice my size too. Having been out of school for so long, most of them didn't know how to answer questions or even do sums, and they resented a little fellow like me being good at most kinds of schoolwork. When we did an assignment in class, the boys in back of me naturally wanted to see my work. They didn't even have to ask; they had only to give me a certain look and I got the message.

These fellows knew I was gentle at heart, and when I passed down their street on my way home from school they would be out on the veranda waiting for me, making disparaging remarks about my appearance. They would start with my hair and work their way gradually down to my feet, and I used to get upset.

My mother was duly sympathetic. "You are a nice-looking boy," she reassured me. "What do they know? Don't listen to them."

That was gratifying but not very helpful, so I went to my grandmother. "Granny, what shall I do?"

"Well," she said, "there are two ways to deal with this kind of situation. One is to remember that what they are saying is untrue, and just repeat your mantram and ignore them. After a while, when they see that you're not bothered, they'll stop."

This too was not what I was looking for. "What's the other way, Granny?"

"The other way," she said, "is for me to take care of it for you."

I said, "Let's try your way."

So we did. Granny never lost her temper, but she had a way of speaking that made even brave men prefer to face a sword. To this day I don't know what she told those boys, but ever after there was an awed respect in their manner and they never bothered me again.

I tell such stories on myself whenever people say, "Oh, it's easy for you to say 'forgive and forbear'; that's your nature." Not at all. I was not born like my Granny, utterly impervious to deprecation. Harsh, taunting words used to hurt me deeply. But gradually I absorbed her unshakable security, based on the sure awareness that the Lord is ever present in our heart of hearts. "The Lord is with me; I shall not fear."

Interestingly enough, I had a cousin who solved this problem an utterly different way. He actually enjoyed courting trouble, because he knew he was good at dealing with it. So where I went out of my way to avoid the bigger boys, my cousin made a point of swaggering down their street, daring them to do so much as raise an eyebrow. They never bothered him either.

"To practice nonviolence in mundane matters is to

know its true value. It is to bring heaven upon earth." Gandhi is claiming in all humility that he doesn't live on earth; he lives in heaven. And it is a heaven in which all of us can dwell when we lose the capacity to feel ill will no matter what the provocation.

When we meet someone with this capacity for mercy, something changes in the depths of our unconscious. Those who merely touched the hem of Jesus' garment, the apostles tell us, received a gift of peace. I believe it was William James who observed that when we meet a saint, a little of our "native meanness" dies. To be hostile is more difficult after that; to be forgiving is more natural. The more we love such a person, the more possibilities open up in our own mind to become merciful, like a window opening inch by inch into deeper awareness.

The scriptures of all religions say that those who tap the reservoir of mercy within eventually become a river of love, which no adversary or adversity can stop. What is the reason for that power? The explanation is simple: whenever you give love to somebody who doesn't know how to love, you educate that person. Even the most insecure and most embittered among us cannot resist for long a person who gives out pure, unconditional love. "Behold the Lamb of God," exclaims John the Baptist, "which taketh away the sin of the world!"

An ancient Sanskrit saying, *"Ahimsa paramo dharma,"* states categorically that nonviolence is the highest law of life. All other laws arise out of it. That is the meaning and significance of mercy in the loftiest sense of the word. If we refer all our decisions, large and small, to this one supreme law, we will get the answers to every raging question of our day.

Gandhi came to this same conclusion. "During my half a century of experience, I have not yet come across one situation when I had to say that I was helpless, that I had no remedy in terms of nonviolence." That is why he is much, much more than just the father of the Indian nation; he is a beacon light to the modern world and to generations yet unborn.

"I am an irrepressible optimist," Gandhi continues. "My optimism rests on my belief in the infinite possibilities of the individual to develop nonviolence. The more you develop it in your own being, the more infectious it becomes, till it overwhelms your surroundings and by and by might oversweep the world." Whenever we forgive unkindness, we are passing on this infection of mercy of which Gandhi speaks. In the heart of every human being lies a noble response to anyone who will neither retaliate nor retreat: a deep, intuitive recognition that here is someone who sees in us all the inalienable good in human nature. That is the source of our unfathomable response to Jesus, to the Buddha, to Teresa of Avila and Francis of Assisi, and of course to Gandhi himself.

"I have known from early youth," Gandhi says, giving away his native genius for love,

> that nonviolence is not a cloistered virtue to be practiced
> by the individual for his peace and final salvation, but it
> is a rule of conduct for the whole of society, if it is to live
> consistently with human dignity and make progress
> towards the attainment of peace, for which it has been
> yearning for ages past. One cannot be nonviolent in
> one's own circle and violent outside.

This knocks the bottom out of claims by governments that they are waging righteous wars, wars to make the world safe for peace. When we are violent in one sphere of life, we kindle violence everywhere we reach.

The economist Ruth Sivard, in her annual *World Military and Social Expenditures*, reminds us how far we have traveled from this law of mercy. In 1987, she reports, the nations of the world spent 930 billion dollars on their military forces. If Jesus were here to see this year of our Lord 1989, he would ask us bluntly: When millions of children are going hungry, how can we go on wasting more than one and a half million dollars a minute on the machinery of war?

The people of the United States and the Soviet Union combined – very resourceful, gifted people, you will agree – "have," Ruth Sivard writes, "only 11 percent of the world's population, but in 1985 they accounted for 23 percent of the world's armed forces, 60 percent of the military expenditures, more than 80 percent of the weapons research, and 97 percent of all nuclear warheads and bombs." If these two nations would only join hands and work together to relieve misery around the world, there would be no more burden of starving billions; every technological obstacle could be removed.

If this sounds naive, I would remind you that thinkers as hardheaded as Carl Sagan and George Kennan, a veteran diplomat of the Cold War, have recently made similar pleas. Neither side would lose anything by this joint effort; in fact, both sides would gain: not only from a safer globe, but from relief from the increasingly crippling economic burden of a war economy. All that is necessary is for ordinary people like you and me to make mercy on a global scale a top priority of our lives. The unknown mystic who left us the *Theologica Germanica* advises that we should "fain be to the Eternal Goodness what his own hand is to a man." It might begin with examining our means of livelihood, refusing any job that threatens life.

There are plenty of challenges to mercy right around us, here in the wealthiest country on earth, and everyone can find some way to help. I learned this from Gandhi. People often do not realize that most of Gandhi's efforts to free India were spent not on marches and demonstrations but on improving the lot of the poor. He traveled all over the subcontinent asking each of us, even children, to make some contribution. He was so successful that today all over India there are modern hospitals for women and children, named after his wife, Kasturbai. Those who can afford to pay give what they can; for those who cannot, treatment is free.

Mercy teaches that all of us in this world are on the same side. First World, Communist bloc, Third World, rich nations and poor, underdeveloped and over-developed, all are ultimately in the same camp. In the opposite camp are war, violence, famine, disease, ignorance, superstition, and the degraded environment that threatens us all. These are what we should be waging all-out war against; if we fail to fight them, we shall surely perish. And instead, we make war on each other! As Buckminster Fuller used to put it, we are all traveling together on a spaceship, this endangered earth. With our ship in such danger, it is so tragically senseless to fight each other and try to knock more holes in the hull.

★

Blessed are the merciful, for they shall receive mercy. It is at the time of death that we receive the final gift of a life of mercy, a life we have lived for all.

Below the surface of consciousness, we can speak roughly of two grand domains. What I call the personal unconscious is the region in which our personal problems arise, shaped by the conditioning of what we have thought, done, and experienced in the past. During the first half of meditation, by digging deeper and deeper into consciousness, we learn to traverse this region, which brings the resolution of most of our personal problems.

This formidable achievement can seem like the end of the spiritual journey, and many have taken it as such. But beyond the personal unconscious stretch the limitless reaches of the collective unconscious, which lies below everything that is personal and separate. Here in these unfathomable depths lies the answer to the mystery of death.

In these dark realms, which have never before been

penetrated by the light of our conscious mind, our image of ourself begins to change as the infinite resources of the unconscious come into our hands. Slowly, without even meaning to, we begin to lose our fear of death. This is an amazing realization; for as Jung says, at these depths the fear of death is written in the hearts of all. Yet it is in these depths that we discover experientially what we may have hoped or believed, but never *known:* that death is not the end for anyone. It is only a gateway, a passage to another state of being. More important, we see that at the very core of ourselves we are neither body nor mind but that small spark in the soul, "uncreated and uncreatable," which can never die.

In the Sanskrit scriptures death is called our friend, because it is awareness of death that gives meaning to life and prompts us to search for what is deathless. Without this awareness, we let life slip by as if it could last forever. Every day time is robbing us of our vitality and of our cherished ideals; we have not a minute to waste in selfish, separate pursuits. When we take this fact of life to heart, we know death to be our loyal friend, always prodding us on toward self-realization.

Against the backdrop of reincarnation, the Tibetan mystics have a picturesque way of describing what happens to personality after the body is shed. I always emphasize that if we live rightly today, there is no need to worry about the next life at all, let alone the influences of the past. But even if we do not believe in reincarnation, these Tibetan theories give a helpful perspective on doing our best here and now. At death, they say, the soul enters a kind of cosmic waiting room called Bardo, where we get a certain time for "R and R" – rest and recuperation – before going on to our next life. These two Rs are our first priority. After being knocked about on the freeway of human existence, we need a chance to recover from the wounds we have both suffered and inflicted. Otherwise we will not be in good shape to learn from our next life, which is the point of being reborn.

But two other Rs are equally important. After rest and recuperation, our next priority in Bardo is reflection. We live in a compassionate universe, and everybody is expected to learn something from life each time around. Bardo gives us a chance for "emotion recollected in tranquility": to review our past and ask ourselves in detachment, "Why did I do such foolish things? Why didn't I do more for other people? What so possessed my attention that I forgot to seek to realize God?" Such questions can be painful, but their purpose is not to punish or torture us. We need to learn from past mistakes what to do and what not to do in order to make our life better the next time around.

Then comes the last R: resolution. "Next time," we say, "I am not going to make these same mistakes, whatever the temptation. I am going to remember what life is for." With this high resolve we are ready to come into life again, where we will be born into just the right context for facing the same trials with new wisdom and courage. That new life, for almost everybody, will be a little better than the last. In particular, if we have been meditating sincerely and following spiritual disciplines, all the momentum of our search will be carried over to our next life. The very fact that you are reading a book like this, these mystics would say, is part of that momentum: you are picking up where you left off last.

Death is a kind of major surgery which every creature has to undergo. Body and mind are severed, and awareness of all that makes up our separate, individual personality is cut away. Without preparation or understanding, this experience can be as painful as crashing headlong into an immovable wall. The only thing that can get us through this wall is the unshakable faith that our deepest Self does not ever die.

Every time we meditate, we can be said to be rehearsing for this moment of surgery, learning that we are not the body but the deathless Self. More than that, we are uniting our passions into a force powerful enough to penetrate the wall of death. At life's last ebb, the immense power of this unified desire can pour into repetition of the Holy Name, which becomes a lifeline we can hold on to while the body is shed.

I have sat by the deathbed of more than one devoted friend and seen this lifeline stretch deep below the conscious level, where it enables us to hold on to the Lord long after awareness of the outside world is gone. Physical trauma is still there, of course. But panic is gone, the panic of loss and self-dissolution, and the fear of the unknown which so fills the human heart with anguish. We know that our story is not ended, and if we have lived in mercy we know for certain that the next chapter will be richer and more fulfilling than the last. David showed this depth of faith in lines that teach us what this Beatitude means: "Surely goodness and mercy shall follow me all the days of my life, and I shall dwell in the house of the Lord forever."

CHAPTER 8
Peacemaking

*Blessed are the peacemakers, for they shall be
called the children of God.*

"PEACE," ACCORDING TO SPINOZA, "is not an
absence of war. It is a virtue, a state of mind, a disposition
for benevolence, trust, and justice."

From this one quotation, you can see how far beyond
politics the mystics' definition of peace goes. If peace
would only be approached as "a virtue, a disposition," the
balance of terror in which most nations on earth hang
would soon vanish. Arms limitation treaties are a necessary first step; but even if all weapons were to disappear
from the earth, Spinoza might tell us today, that would
not guarantee peace. We must actively cultivate peace as a
virtue, trying to make it a permanent state of mind.

Good people around the globe today are concerned
about taking the external steps necessary to promote
peace, but if we want a lasting solution we must search
deeper, into this largely ignored dimension within ourselves. If we acknowledge the relevance of this dimension,

we can hope to do away with war; if we continue to ignore it, no external measure can be of lasting help.

There is a vital connection, the mystics assure us, between the peace or violence in our minds and the conditions that exist outside. When our mind is hostile, it sees hostility everywhere, and we act on what we see. If we could somehow attach a monitor to the mind, we would see the indicator swing into a red danger zone whenever consciousness is agitated by forces like anger and self-will. Acting in anger is not just the result of an agitated mind; it is also a cause, provoking retaliation from others and further agitation in our own mind. If negative behavior becomes habitual, we find ourselves chronically in a negative frame of mind and continually entangled in pointless conflicts – just the opposite of peaceful and pacifying.

"A disposition for benevolence." What a remarkable psychologist is this Spinoza! Millions of people get angry every day over trifles; when this goes on and on, the mind develops a disposition for anger. It doesn't really need a reason to lose its temper; anger is its chronic state. But we should never look on angry people as inherently angry. They are simply people whose minds have been conditioned to get angry, usually because they cannot get their own way. Instead of benevolence, they have developed a habit of hostility. For peace, Spinoza tells us, we need only turn that habit around.

In order to do effective peace work, to reconcile individuals, communities, or countries, we have to have peace in our mind. If we pursue peace with anger and animosity, nothing can be stirred up but conflict. In the end, the tide of violence we see rising day by day can be traced not to missiles or tanks but to what builds and uses those missiles and tanks: the minds of individual men and women. There is where the battle for peace has to be won. As the UNESCO constitution puts it, "Since war is born in the minds of men, it is in the minds of men that we have to erect the ramparts of peace." A familiar truth, but one we still have not learned.

How can peace ever emerge from actions prompted by suspicion, anger, and fear? By their very nature, such actions provoke retaliation in kind. If Mahatma Gandhi were here to look behind the scenes at our international summit meetings and accords, he would say compassionately, "Yes, these are a good beginning, but you need to follow them up. You're sitting at a peace table, but there is no peace in your hearts."

I knew hundreds of students in India during Gandhi's long struggle for independence from the British Empire. I met hundreds more in Berkeley during the turbulent sixties, when students all over the country were honestly trying to work for peace. I watched their relationships with one another, especially with those who differed with them, and I saw that these relationships often were not harmonious. If your mind is not trained to make peace at home, Gandhi would ask, how can you hope to promote peace on a larger scale? Until we develop enough mastery over our thinking process to maintain a peaceful attitude in all circumstances – a "disposition for benevolence" – we are likely to vacillate when the going gets tough, without even realizing what has happened.

After some of those demonstrations that were capturing headlines, I used to remind my friends that agitating for peace and actually bringing it about are not necessarily the same. Stirring up passions, provoking animosity, and polarizing opposition may sometimes produce short-term gains, but it cannot produce long-term beneficial results because it only clouds minds on both sides. Progress comes only from opening others' eyes and hearts, and that can happen only when people's minds are calmed and their fears allayed. It is not enough if your political will is peaceful; your entire will should be peaceful. It is not enough if one part of your personality says "No more war"; the whole of your personality should be nonviolent.

One of these students told me with chagrin that he once found himself using his fists to promote peace. Things just got out of control. "How did that happen?" he asked incredulously. "I never would have dreamed of doing such a thing!"

I told him not to judge himself too harshly: after all, the will to strike back is part of our biological heritage. When push comes to shove, unless we have trained ourselves to harness our anger – to put it to work to heal the situation instead of aggravating it – it is monumentally difficult for most of us to resist the impulse to retaliate.

In situations like these, one first aid measure is to leave the scene and take a mantram walk. The force of your anger will drive the mantram deeper, bringing you closer to the day when you can rise above those fierce negative forces. Each repetition of the mantram, especially in trying moments, is like money put into a trust account in the Bank of Saint Francis. One day that account will mature, and you will become an instrument of peace. You may have no idea of what capacity you will serve in: after all, Francis himself hadn't a clue to the direction his life would take when he began placing stone upon stone to restore the chapel at San Damiano. But you can be sure that the banker within will provide you with enough compassion, security, and wisdom to make a creative contribution to solving the problems of our times.

The mystics are tremendous psychologists. It has taken more than two thousand years for secular civilization to begin to accept that penetrating aphorism of Ruysbroeck, which expresses a central tenet of spiritual psychology: "We behold that which we are, and we are that which we behold." If we have an angry mind, we will see life as full of anger; if we have a suspicious mind, we will see causes for suspicion all around: precisely because we and the world are not separate.

When suspicion lurks in our hearts, we can never quite trust others. Most of us go about like medieval knights, carrying a shield wherever we go in case we have to ward off a blow. After a day of carrying a shield around at the office, who wouldn't be exhausted? We take the shield to bed with us for seven or eight hours and wake up wondering why we still feel worn out. And of course, with a big piece of iron on one arm, we find it hard to embrace a friend or offer a hand in help. What began as a simple defense mechanism becomes a permanent, crippling appendage.

Statesmen are no different: they too are human beings, albeit with a most important job. When they go to the conference table, they too carry their shields. Worse, their suspicions may prompt them to carry a sword in the other hand, or to sit down with a clenched fist – which, as Indira Gandhi once said, makes it impossible to shake hands. Yet that is just how most nations today come to the peace table, desiring a meeting of minds but prepared to fight to get their own way. They don't expect peace, they expect trouble: and expecting trouble, I sometimes think, is the best way of inviting it.

When we change our way of seeing, we begin to live in a different world. If we approach others with respect and trust, with a great deal of patience and internal toughness, we will slowly begin to find ourselves in a compassionate universe where change for the better is always possible, because of the core of goodness we see in the hearts of others. That is how I see the world today. It is not that I fail to see suffering and sorrow. But I understand the laws of life and see its unity everywhere, so I feel at home wherever I go.

Wernher von Braun, the pioneer of astronautics, once

said that for those who know its laws, outer space is not the hostile environment it seems but very friendly. Traveling in space is as safe as sitting in our living rooms – so long as we understand the rules of space and abide by them. Similarly, those who know the laws of the mind live in peace and security even in the midst of storms. They choose not to hate because they know that hatred only breeds hatred, and they work for peace because they know that preparation for war can only lead to war. When people wonder if programs like "Star Wars" will work, I reply, "That is the last question we should ask. The first question is, Can wrong means ever lead to right ends?" Can we ever prepare for war and get peace?

"One day," said Martin Luther King, Jr., "we must come to see that peace is not merely a distant good but a means by which we arrive at that good. We must pursue peaceful ends through peaceful means." In his speech accepting the Nobel Peace Prize in 1964, King said:

> Nonviolence is the answer to the crucial political and moral questions of our time; the need for man to overcome oppression and violence without resorting to oppression and violence.
>
> Man must evolve for all human conflict a method which rejects revenge, aggression and retaliation. The foundation of such a method is love.

It is a living law, a law governing all of life, that ends and means are indivisible. Right means cannot help but lead to right ends; and wrong means – waging war, for example, to ensure peace – cannot help but result in wrong ends. Gandhi went to the extent of telling us to use right means and not worry about the outcome at all; the very laws of our existence will ensure that the outcome of our efforts will be beneficial in the long run. The only question we have to ask ourselves is, Am I giving everything I can to bring about peace – at home, on the streets, in this country, around the world? If enough of us start acting on this question, peace is very near.

What we do with our hands, the mystics say, is a direct expression of the forces in our minds. Even our technology is an expression of some of our deepest desires. The crisis of industrial civilization, which could create the conditions of paradise on this earth and yet threatens to destroy it, only reflects the deeper division in our hearts. "Our nuclear buildup isn't something unique," says Joseph Chilton Pearce, an author and former humanities teacher, "but it is the clearest and most inescapable end-result, or final expression, of our whole current mode of life and way of thinking." Instead of blaming our problems on some intrinsic flaw in human nature, we must squarely take responsibility for our actions as human beings capable of rational thought.

But this view has a heartening side: if it is we who got ourselves into this habit of suspicion, we have the capacity to get ourselves out too. Simply to understand this is a great step in the right direction, where we do not sit back and bemoan our irrational "animal" behavior but accept that our nuclear-threatened world is an expression of our way of thinking and feeling. The terrible dilemma which we face is the ultimate result of our mode of life, our motivation, the kind of relationships we have cultivated with other countries, our whole philosophy of life. Here again is Martin Luther King, Jr.:

> I refuse to accept the idea that the "isness" of man's present nature makes him morally incapable of reaching up for the "oughtness" that forever confronts him. . . .
> I refuse to accept the cynical notion that nation after nation must spiral down a militaristic stairway into the hell of nuclear destruction. I believe that unarmed truth and unconditional love will have the final word in reality.

In this presumably sophisticated world, it is considered naive to be trusting. In that case I am proud to say that I must be one of the naivest people on earth. If someone has let me down a dozen times, I will still trust that person for the thirteenth time. Trust is a measure of your depth of faith in the nobility of human nature, of your depth of love for all. If you expect the worst from someone, the worst is what you will usually get. Expect the best and people will respond: sometimes swiftly, sometimes not so swiftly, but there is no other way.

When statesmen and politicians view other nations through the distorting lens of hatred and suspicion, the policies they come up with only keep the fires of hostility smoldering. "Hate those who hate us – and, if possible, threaten them as well": this is scarcely a path to peace; it is only the path of stimulus and response. Jesus gave us a path that matches means to ends: "Do good to them that hate you." This should be the basis even of foreign policy. There is no surer route to building trust and dispelling fear, the prime mover behind all arms races.

Because we see as we are, not only are our policies backward but our priorities are upside down. We long for peace but work for war, often under the label of "defense." That is where the time, talent, and resources of some of our "best and brightest" go. Joseph Chilton Pearce again is direct and to the point:

> From where does our incredibly sophisticated arsenal of destruction come? From the Pentagon? They couldn't make a paper airplane. Our instruments of destruction come from our "finest intellects" – the academic-scientific community who, with one side of their mouth, bemoan the stupid politicians, and with the other, beg for DOD [Department of Defense] grants, money, fame and Nobels, by which they give the "warlords" their swords. Withdraw the supporting think-systems from

Harvard, M.I.T., U. Cal., Stanford, Caltech, and so on, and the power of the warlords would disappear.

Being a scientist is a tremendous responsibility. If just half a dozen top scientists from institutions like these should withdraw their support from the war effort, it would be a great contribution to peace. Instead, some of our best scientific thinking and technological talent stays with war. No one has appraised the result better than General Omar Bradley, whom I quoted at the beginning of this book. "We have grasped the mystery of the atom," he says,

> and rejected the Sermon on the Mount. . . . The world has achieved brilliance without conscience. Ours is a world of nuclear giants and ethical infants. We know more about war than we do about peace, more about killing than we know about living.

Strong words, but we need a strong reminder of how ridiculous our values have become. General Bradley's language reminds me of an episode I once saw in a run-of-the-mill Indian movie, in which a simple villager goes to Bombay for the first time. When he comes back, his friends ask him what he thought of the big city. "Such tall buildings," he says, "and such small people." Very perceptive. That is our world, "nuclear giants and ethical infants."

When I first arrived in this country, at the Port of New York, friends took me to Times Square to ooh and aah at the architecture. I went, but I didn't ooh and aah. That puzzled them. "Oh, you're just acting blasé," they said. "You know you've never seen a skyscraper before. Aren't you impressed?"

"Buildings don't impress me," I confessed. "People do. I may not have seen a skyscraper, but I have met and walked with a man to match the Himalayas, Mahatma

Gandhi. Show me someone big like that and you'll see how impressed I can be."

Do you remember the movie in which Charlie Chaplin goes on looking for the top of a skyscraper until finally he topples over backward? That is not going to happen to me, and it should not happen to you. We should never be impressed by something just because it is big, whether it is a big building or a big bomb. These are not the signs of an advanced civilization, and they have nothing to do with progress and growth. One real "ethical giant" is of much more significance in history.

I believe it was Prince Edward, the Duke of Windsor, who went on a shooting expedition when visiting India many years ago and managed to get separated from the rest of his party. Finally the others started firing into the air to make their position known. "Ah!" Edward exclaimed when he heard the shots. "The sound of civilization!"

Today, instruments of destruction have become so deadly that however sophisticated the technology, nations which concentrate on developing, selling, and stockpiling weapons might be said to be losing their claim to civilization. We can make a rough map of the truly civilized world: the bigger the arsenal of nuclear weapons, the weaker the claim to being a civilized power. To be truly civilized, a government must subscribe to the highest law: respect for life, to the point of being unwilling to kill or to cause others to kill.

I am a very hard-nosed person. I do not get impressed by speeches and rallies and media coverage about arms control. How much are we willing to give, and give up, to make peace a reality? That is the question. It is not just what we say and write but how we order our lives – how we apportion our time, distribute our resources, and behave in everyday relationships – that counts for peace. "We rage against 'forces' over which we have no control,"

Pearce says. "But control would require effort, and our efforts go to self-comfort, personal benefit, and living the good life."

"I see no way out of this dilemma," says the veteran statesman George Kennan, who has lived through thaws and freezes in the Cold War since 1945,

> other than by a bold and sweeping departure, a departure that would cut surgically through the exaggerated anxieties, the self-indentured nightmares, and the sophisticated mathematics of destruction in which we have all been entangled over these recent years, and would permit us to move with courage and decision to the heart of the problem.

Kennan is talking about nothing less than a complete reversal of our ways of thinking. Both Washington and Moscow peer out on the world through a curtain of suspicion, mistrust, and fear which distorts vision and allows no other way of seeing. How can peace ever come in such a climate? To have peace we must learn to see where we stand on common ground, beginning with certain basic truths: that people in all countries are essentially the same, whether their governments are communist or capitalist, and that neither of the superpowers threatens the other as much as the arms race threatens us all.

To change course like this, we human beings have to learn to talk to each other even when our opinions differ. And that requires respect. Nothing closes communication more swiftly and effectively than this business of painting the other side with an all-black brush. If it were not so tragic, it would be amusing to compare how often the same comments are hurled like rockets by both sides. Each claims to be innocent of all wrong and views the other as the epitome of evil.

Citizen exchanges can do wonders to dissolve such barriers on the personal level. It pleases me very much to see that high school and university exchange programs are beginning to include teachers and students from China and the Soviet Union. We can send more students, more scholars, more artists and dancers and musicians and athletes, to countries with whom we differ politically; they do more for peace than most politicians. It is more than a quarter of a century since I first came to this country on the Fulbright exchange program as a professor of English literature, and I feel I am still fulfilling the spirit of my exchange. I still work for international peace – not by giving lectures on a few dusty texts, but by dispelling mistrust and suspicion in every way I can.

Rich or poor, powerful or not so powerful, ally or antagonist or nonaligned, every nation needs help and understanding if the world is to get out of this nuclear trap, for nuclear arms are no longer exclusive to superpowers. We must begin to see this massive threat as an opportunity to build a new world – one world, not divided by nationalistic rivalries – or else we shall perish by our own politics.

This is an opportunity for every one of us. Our children face right now the dreadful reality that life as we know it can be wiped out in half an hour's time. If we remember this always, it will bring the motivation to work hard for our children, for their life, for their world.

Our children deserve to grow up in a peaceful world, and it is our responsibility to do everything we can to see that they get the chance. This is why our schools are so important – and let me repeat, the home is the most important school of all. Teachers should not have to declare themselves "educators for social responsibility"; that is their role. I want to see that hundreds of millions of children understand this basic choice and have the opportunity to make it. When they reach voting age they should be able to tell anyone running for office, "If you support war, you are not going to get my vote. You must stand squarely and unequivocally for peace; then I'll see that you get in." If enough of us say that and mean it, the struggle is as good as won.

One very serious obstacle to children growing up with this point of view was pointed out a few years ago on the front page of the *Christian Science Monitor* during the Christmas shopping season. The headline read, "Toy Companies Ride Military Wave and Watch Kids Catch It." How early the seeds of violence are sown! Toys are not neutral; they influence children's thinking and emotions, for better or worse. When my young friend Christina was two, she used to bring her dolls with her to the dinner table. When I asked her, "How is your little one today?" she would say, "She has a cold." "Does she wake you up by crying at night?" "No, she just sleeps." Those dolls were real to her. Children need toys that are fun, but they also need toys that inspire them, toys that make them more sensitive to other people and creatures. So many toys today do just the opposite.

The *Monitor* article went on to supply illustrations: "Tricycles with bazookas attached; guns that shoot beams of infrared light at the opponent. Dolls with bad breath, or those with controversial messages, like Grace the pro-life doll and Nomad the Arab terrorist. These and other toys are on more wish-lists than ever before." Children cannot be held responsible for putting violent, tawdry stuff on their Christmas lists. It is we adults who are responsible: well-intentioned parents, grandparents, relatives, and friends; television programmers and media manipulators; and especially those who make and sell whatever promises to bring in a profit, regardless of the values it may represent.

Every parent can play a useful role in reversing this trend – particularly every mother. When you give toys to children, or allow them to buy them for themselves, you have to consider that you are not just giving them something to entertain them; you are giving them an instrument that may influence their thinking and living for decades.

Of course, big money is involved in toys today. Isn't it involved in most of our big problems? "Controversy" over such toys, the *Monitor* continues, "has not hurt sales. Laser Tag, which is number five on *Toy and Hobby World* magazine's most-popular lists, is expected to bring in a hundred million in sales this year." (Laser Tag involves shooting at opponents with a light-gun; when a person is hit, his target gives off an electronic death rattle.) That is a hundred million from the pockets of parents. The president of the company that makes Laser Tag says that the toy merely "puts a high-tech spin on a time-honored game." Laser Tag, he says, "is a vehicle to bring children together." It brings them together in insensitivity to violence, and it fosters the thinking that perpetuates war.

Developments like these will bear bitter fruit in the lives of our children, and that is why every parent has a responsibility to think about this issue, write about it, and speak about it to others. I admit, this is undramatic work. Nobody is likely to give you recognition or put you on the front page of the newspaper. But this is the kind of work that expresses real commitment to peace. If a thousand or so mothers and fathers speak up on this issue, within ten years we will see a completely different kind of toy market in this country. Toys that help, inspire, and strengthen while they entertain are quite within human reach.

But the surest way to educate children for peace is through our personal example. This is the responsibility of every one of us – not just parents, but everyone who has contact with young people. Children quietly absorb what we teach through our actions and attitudes, so there is no more powerful way to show them what the silent power of a peaceful mind and a loving heart can do.

One of the things that impressed me deeply about Gandhi, for example, was his ability to calm a violent crowd. I don't think anywhere in this country are you likely to see crowds like those in India. You got an idea of them in the film *Gandhi:* tens of thousands of people gathered in one place; and in those days they were sometimes in no mood to be nonviolent. Often Gandhi stood before an angry crowd clamoring for retaliation, "an eye for an eye." I have seen him quiet them just by raising his hand, and with one reminder make them stop to think: "An eye for an eye only makes the whole world blind." After a few minutes we would all go away calmer and braver, having tasted a little of the peace that was in the heart of this spiritual giant. The eyes, the voice, and the gestures of such a person communicate with people even from a distance and bring them peace.

We may not be called on to face multitudes or to calm the storms of nations, but we can all begin by calming storms in the teacup of our homes. This is the only way we can help our children to grow up in peace and security. We may not have found a world at peace ourselves, but it is quite within our power to create one for the next generation – if we will only make peace, rather than personal profit or pleasure, the first priority in our lives.

Family relationships are so important that we cannot afford to relegate them to secondary status, putting children or partner after our job and income and status. Nothing is more important than the children of our nation, our only essential resource; and each of us, remember, is their teacher by our example. Every morning after meditation I ask myself what I would be without my grandmother, my spiritual teacher. I might have acquired a well-trained intellect, but I would never have learned how to train my mind, the most precious skill on earth.

★

No one can be blamed for thinking, "This is out of my reach! Human nature is, after all, only human. Isn't survival of the fittest a biological imperative? Isn't violence part of our very nature?" Most scientists would agree. "What I think I know of the history of our species," says a distinguished professor of animal behavior and Nobel laureate from Oxford, Niko Tinbergen, "makes me afraid that in the struggle between rational, long-term insight and nonrational, short-term motivation, it will be the latter that will win."

No one would argue that this fear is groundless. At the same time, biologists sometimes need to be reminded that human beings are not the same as animals. My body is that of an animal, but I am not my body. The spark that burns in me, in you, is lit from the fire of heaven.

I respect research which draws on animal physiology to help us learn more about physical health, but when it comes to drawing conclusions about human character on the basis of animal studies, I draw the line. The human personality, though it has fascinating correlates in the brain and throughout the rest of the body, is not physical and cannot be biologically explained; and the core of personality, the Self, is not even mental but wholly spiritual. Nothing the physical sciences can discover, therefore, can limit what you or I can become. An animal may have little choice in pursuing its food, comfort, and survival; but you and I have the capacity to choose to go against profit and pleasure and every other conditioned motivation for the sake of others, or simply for the sake of an ideal.

This is a supremely human trait, yet we can see it burgeoning even in animals that are highly advanced in evolution. The elephant, for example, is an extremely powerful creature that will not knowingly harm any other animal.

The female elephant considers all calves her own and will protect all the young of the herd from harm at the risk of her life. I have seen a huge elephant step out of the way to avoid crushing a tiny frog that you and I would probably never notice. And not long ago I read of a dog that escaped from a burning building and then ran back inside to rescue the little girl it loved. Even when it comes to animal behavior, then, I do not always agree that creatures are biologically determined to behave selfishly, motivated solely by short-term gratification.

When I was a professor in India, I used to see learned papers reporting on experiments on how rats behave when put under pressure. I used to tell my students, "You're not rats!" Don't ever put yourselves in the category of rodents. Theirs is a different world, and I wonder sometimes how deep our understanding of that world goes when we observe an animal doing certain things and draw conclusions about what it means.

So much in the field of human psychology is based on animal experiments that we should not be surprised when research reports give a pessimistic picture of human motivation. It has been said that it is scholarly to be pessimistic: if you are optimistic, you must not have done your homework very well. If that is true, I am no scholar. I am incorrigibly, though realistically, optimistic, because I know that beneath even the most selfish, violent behavior there lies in every human personality a spring of goodness, flowing from the sea of love that is the Self.

In fact, this "disposition for benevolence, trust, and justice" which Spinoza defines as peacemaking flows from that very aspect of our nature which is *not* part of an animal heritage, but distinctly human. It is a skill, a skill in thinking, and like any physical skill – swimming, skiing, gymnastics, tennis – it can be learned by anyone who is willing to practice.

This approach should have immense appeal today. We know how to teach computer programming and coronary care nursing. The mystics tell us simply to do the same with peace: to approach it as a skill which can be systematically learned if we apply ourselves to the task. If there is no peace in the world, in our communities, or in our homes, it is not because war is built into our genes; it is because we have no idea of the requisite mental skills of peacemaking. With no way to learn these skills, we move farther from peace every day.

When we first set out to learn this "disposition for benevolence," of course, the going will be rough. The conditioning of stimulus and response, "an eye for an eye," is strong. But as meditation deepens, you find there is a fierce satisfaction in letting go of your own way so that things can go someone else's way instead. Gradually you develop a habit of goodness, a hang-up for kindness, a positive passion for the welfare of others. In terms of emotional engineering, you are using the mind's enormous capacity for passion to develop the power to put other people first: and not just verbally, but in your thoughts and actions as well. Eventually kindness becomes spontaneous, second nature; it no longer requires effort. There is nothing sentimental about this quality, either; kindness can be as tough as nails.

We can see in the life of Gandhi how he developed this disposition for kindness. Even as a young man in South Africa, he wrote that he was unable to understand how a person could get satisfaction out of treating others with cruelty. Yet this attitude was not enough in itself to prevent him from reacting with anger when provoked. It took years of practice to drive this conviction so deep that it became an integral part of his character, consciousness, and conduct.

Why do we feel we have to lash out against others? The mystics give a very compassionate explanation: because we have uneducated minds. If the mind acts unruly, that is simply because we have not put it through school.

This kind of education is scarcely available anywhere in the world today. I have had the privilege of being associated with great universities both in this country and in India, and I deeply wish that in addition to educating the heads of their students, they could teach the skills that enable us to educate our minds and hearts. It is what we know in the heart, not in the head, that matters most; for what we believe, we become. "As a man thinketh in his heart," the Bible says, "so is he."

For most of us, intellectual knowledge has very little say in the choices that shape our lives. You may know in painful detail about the harmful consequences of smoking, but if you have ever smoked, you know how shallow that knowledge is when measured against the power of habit and desire. I have seen a physician pondering X-ray films of a diseased lung with a lighted cigarette between his lips.

Similarly, you may know from bitter experience how destructive anger can be, but that makes it no easier to keep your temper the next time something provokes you. The reason is simple: there is very little connection between the intellect and the will. Intellectual knowledge is on the surface of consciousness; addictions, urges, and conditioned cravings arise deep in the unconscious mind. And the vast majority of us cannot bring our will to bear in the unconscious; even in waking life, the will may have little to do.

When you reach a certain depth in meditation, however, all this changes. You gain access to the will even below the surface of awareness, which means you can actually get underneath a craving or negative emotion and pull it out. This is the most challenging adventure life offers: to tunnel slowly under a craving for tobacco or alcohol, overeating or drugs, and remove it like a weed.

After decades of sustained effort, you finally get to the roots of the primordial drives that take their toll on the lives of every one of us: self-will, anger, fear, and greed.

Let me change metaphors to make a practical illustration. All these forces – anger, for example – can be thought of as powerful physical forces like electricity. Electricity can destroy us, but when harnessed, it can also bring us light and warmth. In the same way, we can learn to use anger as a positive force, devoid of any ill feeling, to heal divisions between persons and nations and to find creative solutions to conflicts. When we have gained mastery over our responses, when deepening meditation brings insight and creativity, when will and desire have fused into a passionate determination to act only for the good of all, we have simply to flip a switch to redirect the current into its new channel.

To do this takes a great deal of preparation, of course. The mind has to be trained to listen to you when all it wants to do is turn tail and run, or lash out in retaliation. The muscles of the will have to be made strong enough to reach for that switch when everything in you is screaming, "You're wrong!" This takes a lot of work, but the day will come when, in the heat of a conflict, you will be able to say quietly, "Let's look at this problem together and see what we can do to solve it."

In presenting the connection between meditation and peace, then, I am not advancing moral or ethical arguments. I am presenting the dynamics of acquiring a new disposition of mind. Through the practice of meditation and its allied disciplines, every one of us can become a peacemaker by making "a disposition for benevolence" our natural state: that is, by teaching the mind to be calm and kind.

The purpose of meditation is to bring lasting peace to the mind. This is not a superficial suppression of hostility, but a profound, joyful, enduring peace of mind. It can pervade our consciousness to such an extent, Gandhi says, that even in our dreams we will not feel animosity toward anyone. Imagine! Most of us find it difficult in our waking moments to have love in our hearts always, but such is the power of these tremendous spiritual disciplines that once they are mastered, even in the unconscious no wave of anger will be able to rise.

In fact, this is how your meditation will be tested. You will have been meditating regularly for years, perhaps decades, when someone dear to you bursts out against you in cruel words. It would be only natural for your mind to be so agitated that anger, anguish, vengeful feelings, perhaps nightmares, follow you into your sleep. But Jesus says no. Natural it may be, but not necessary. Hatred does not have to be the human response to hatred. We have the capacity to love and forgive; and if your meditation is really good, these are the forces that will sweep up from the depths of your consciousness in your sleep, healing your heart and releasing new resources for reaching out to the person who has wronged you.

To do this, as Spinoza says, requires a deep trust – trust in the native goodness within others and in ourselves. I was not born with this kind of trust – neither, in fact, was Gandhi – but today, after many years of training my mind, if somebody says something unkind to me it doesn't bother me very much. What does bother me is the other person's state of mind, because I know what sorrow the habit of unkindness brings. It's a wonderful reversal of sensitiveness.

No philosophical conviction can confer this depth of security. It requires some glimpse of the Self, the Lord within, who is one and the same in all. Spinoza uses a medieval phrase for this that appeals to me very much: *sub specie aeternitatis*. Seen from the aspect of eternity, each of us is but a mode of one infinite reality which dwells in the heart of every finite creature. When you are always aware of this deep, underlying unity, how can you be upset by apparent differences? Who can make you feel threatened or insecure? The message of all great religions is the same: Regard everybody as yourself, because everybody *is* you. Whatever others may say or do, you will know that the Lord lives in them, and you will always treat them accordingly.

Yet it is not enough that this core of love is always present. We have to learn to express it, which requires gaining the capacity to say no to the conditioned demands of physical nature. That is why I teach meditation, to bring about this gradual but fundamental change in consciousness. I wait for those moments when somebody tells me, "I don't know how to be kind." I say, "I can teach you – or rather you can teach yourself, through the practice of meditation." Memorize a passage on kindness, on goodness, and then drive it inward every day, deeper and deeper into consciousness. If you persist, you will become that kind, good person on which you meditate; it cannot fail.

The other day I went with a friend to take his car in for minor repairs. The mechanic lay down on his back on his little moving dolly and vanished under the engine, where he could look around and see just what needed to be done: a screw that needed tightening, I suppose, or maybe loosening. This is what we do in meditation. It takes a long, long time to get under the engine that is the mind – and hard work, daring, and a great reservoir of devotion to the task. But no skill is more worth learning. When you get deep in consciousness, you can actually look up at the workings of the mind with wrench in hand. Then transforming anger becomes a mechanical problem; overcoming fears becomes a matter of tightening or loosening a screw.

The only reason we are not able to do this kind of fix-it work is that we have not learned how. There is no school where this skill is taught. Powerful disciplines for training the mind do exist, handed down to us from the great traditions of every religion. Yet they are largely ignored in today's world; in West and East alike, we are in danger of losing this precious legacy.

Augustine, who had a very modern perspective on the workings of the mind, asks pointedly, "I can tell my hand what to do and it will obey me. Why can I not do the same with my mind?" If the mind gets angry and you tell it to calm down, it is likely to retort, "Who do you think you are to talk to me like that? Why should I listen to you?" It's like a gawky teenager protesting, "Dad, you never sent me to school! How can you complain because I can't read?"

I have real sympathy for the untrained mind, so uneducated and illiterate. It is big and powerful but all thumbs, all turmoil and tempestuousness, bumbling through life like a Saint Bernard puppy and knocking everything over. Yet this clumsy creature can be taught anything we care to teach it, if we only have patience and persevere – and once it has learned how to behave, this embarrassing and unpredictable liability becomes our greatest ally. "Neither your father nor your mother," the Buddha says, "neither husband nor wife nor child, can be such a loyal friend as your mind when it has been trained." It will stand by you in all circumstances. When you go among unkind people, your peaceable mind will enable you to be kind to them and quiet their hearts, which is the only peacemaking approach that really works.

All the mind's habits of unkindness can be unlearned. If the mind is coaxed further and further into positive words and actions, the unkind person will gradually think, feel, and act kindly; the unloving person will think, feel, and act out of love. To all who are agitated, insecure, unhappy, there quickly follows peace of mind.

When the mind is trained over a long, long period, you

will not need effort to meet hatred with goodness. Goodness will be your mind's spontaneous response. An educated mind has a very casual style. It has its diploma, so it knows it can stay cool under provocation – which means we lose all fear of anger; we know we will not lose control.

Patanjali, one of the finest teachers of meditation in ancient India, implies that when you live in the presence of someone who will trust you over and over again, you cannot help rising to be worthy of that trust. Gradually you become so tired of letting him down that you become trustworthy.

This does not mean that we should look the other way when someone does something unworthy of him. It means that we must have the inner toughness to hold fast to our faith that there is in that person a core of goodness that does respond to trust and love. Whether between individuals or between nations, without this faith, peace is not possible.

★

If we want to be real peace workers, then, we have to work on removing anger from our personality: not suppressing it, but harnessing it into love poured into concerted action. If we can do this, opportunities for peace work will open up everywhere in our lives. I appreciate the yearning for peace that is expressed in truly nonviolent demonstrations and vigils, but as the Buddha said, those who help the world most are those who help to banish anger, greed, and fear. No one is more active on the path of peace than those who try every day to reduce their own selfish passions and self-will. They may not be participating in demonstrations, but they deserve to be called children of God, for they are true peacemakers, spreading peace everywhere through their daily lives.

Conversely, when someone is being selfish, he or she is actually contributing in a small measure to war. You may refuse to be in the fighting forces, you may be a peace advocate of the most vocal kind, but these things are not enough to make you a peacemaker. I never lay the blame for war at the door of the military. Wherever there is anger, selfishness, greed, or self-will, a foundation for war is being laid, and all of us must accept a share of the blame.

It is this gradual raising of popular consciousness that will bring about peace. We should demand of our politicians that they stand for peace, but we should never look to them to guarantee it; they have vested interests. The military cannot ensure peace because it is conditioned for war. It is ordinary citizens, you and I, who make the final difference. Lisa Peattie, professor of urban anthropology at MIT, puts it persuasively: "The power to move the system must come, I think, from a sort of great popular uprising, a refusal, a mass defense of human life." The former prime minister of Sweden, Olaf Palme, agreed:

It is very unlikely that disarmament will ever take place if it must wait for the initiatives of governments and experts. It will only come about as the expression of the political will of people, in many parts of the world.

I am respectful of governments, but I have no illusion that peace will come through their efforts. It is governments that have got us into this dilemma, with our support; now it is we, the people, who must take the lead in insisting on a wholly different approach. It is not first-strike capacity but first-trust capacity that we should be pursuing with all our might. It would cost a good deal less, and it would release economic and human resources into the bargain. Isn't this the message that Jesus' life conveys? Each one of us, by establishing peace in our minds and practicing it in all our relationships, can hasten the day when peace will reign on earth.

"Some day," said Dwight D. Eisenhower, who was president when I first came to this country, the demand for disarmament by hundreds of millions will, I hope, become so universal and so insistent that no man, no men, can withstand it. We have to mobilize the hundreds of millions; we have to make them understand the choice is theirs. We have to make the young people see to it that they need not be the victims of the Third World War.

Again, these are the words not of a peacenik but of a great general. Eisenhower knew, as every insightful general knows, that if we want peace we cannot count on whoever is sitting in the White House or Number 10 Downing Street or the Kremlin. If each of us, through the example of our own lives, can inspire two more people every year to meditate and to live at peace with those around them, it will have an incalculably great effect in creating a climate of peace. That is my ambition, and that is why I say I am a terribly ambitious man. You and I make peace. You and I make war. It all depends on us.

In other words, if we want to change the world, we have to change ourselves. Unfortunately, that is not where most people begin. Most of the leaders I have met, both here and in India, strike a more familiar tone: "Let me reform you, Diane, and you, George, and of course you, Bob." That is often the reason why well-intentioned efforts to change conditions in other countries fail to get the effects at which they aim. The great spiritual teachers of all religions – Jesus, Saint Francis, Saint Teresa, the Buddha, Mahatma Gandhi – say in refreshing contrast, "Let's start with ourselves."

It is an astonishing truth: there is only one person in the world I can hope to control, and that is myself. I may learn to govern the way I think, but I can never govern the way you think. How much of our behavior reveals that we have not grasped this truth at all! Viewed from this perspective, daily life takes on the qualities of a comedy of errors. I want you to stop being angry, so I get angry with you. I want your mind to be patient when I say something offensive, to be understanding when I say something incomprehensible. I'm always worried about what you are doing and feeling when I should be worrying about my own feelings and behavior. I can only change myself: but in doing that, I do influence how you act too. There is no other way to help a person change.

Yesterday my wife and I had an encounter with a flock of quails. These curious creatures know how to fly, but they prefer not to. When we drive up, they just go on walking right down the middle of the road. It is only when they get desperate, when the fender is a foot or two away, that they bother to use their wings and clatter up together out of the way.

We human beings are much like that. We know how to fly, but we have forgotten. We have come to think of ourselves as plump, pedestrian quails, bipeds without wings. Often it is only after one quail takes off that the others even consider the possibility. One bird suddenly says, "Look! I may be a quail, but I'm in the sky!" Then the others look around and think, "Fancy that! Maybe I can fly too." Two or three others try, and abruptly there is a great flapping of wings and everybody is in the air.

The solution to rampant violence, to international suspicion and the specter of a nuclear nightmare, begins with a challenge to each of us: Change yourself. If you can change yourself, you can reach anybody. We should always remember that there is great hope for the world, because one person changing himself has effects that reach much farther than we see. As Gandhi said, if one man gains spiritually, the whole world gains with him. Wherever there have been beneficial changes in history, that is how they have come about. And we don't have to wait until the other person, the other nation, decides to change. Why don't we change first? Through the practice of meditation, it all lies within our reach.

CHAPTER 9
Desire

*Blessed are they which do hunger and thirst after
righteousness, for they shall be filled.*

I DON'T THINK I have ever come across a more penetrating summary of the human condition than one given
thousands of years ago in the Upanishads, the earliest
source of the Perennial Philosophy yet found:

> You are what your deep, driving desire is.
> As your deep, driving desire is, so is your will.
> As your will is, so is your deed.
> As your deed is, so is your destiny.

Spinoza once said penetratingly that most of us mistake
our desires for decisions. When we think we decide to buy
something, go somewhere, see someone, all too often the
choice is being made not by us, but by unconscious
desires. Unless we develop some capacity to direct our
desires, living in freedom is only a pretty idea.

The intellect, so useful in making decisions on shal-
lower levels, simply cannot operate at the deep level of
desires. All it can do is rationalize actions we have already

been forced to take. That is why even little desires like smoking a cigarette or polishing off two servings of dessert, even when we want to say no to them, can sometimes get the better of us. It is not fair to criticize people for such peccadillos, as if getting addicted were something they chose to do.

In Hindu and Buddhist spiritual psychology, this control of the unconscious is considered almost a kind of magic. That is one connotation of the word *maya:* a kind of cosmic sleight of hand in which the senses cast a spell over us with their promise that if only we indulge them, they will make us happy. Regrettably, they have no power to do anything of the kind. But if we fail to see through their game of illusion and go on giving them what they clamor for, we go through life more and more frustrated, longing to get from sensory experience what it can never give.

I met many young people caught in this game in the sixties, when I was teaching meditation in Berkeley just off Telegraph Avenue – "where the action was." I knew that many of the people coming to hear me were sampling a smorgasbord of drugs. I used to say: "This is a come-as-you-are party. Come with whatever difficulties and addictions you have, learn to meditate, and listen to what the great mystics say about fusing desires and directing them to a supreme goal. Then let us see what happens." Hundreds of them, I am happy to say, gave up smoking and drugs without any direct appeal on my part. When they learned to take the energy that fueled those desires and direct it to goals which have the power to fulfill desires, addictions simply fell away.

I went so far as to tell my meditation class on the Berkeley campus – which numbered a thousand in those days – that Berkeley students had what it takes to understand the spiritual psychology of desire: a good intellect, some measure of sophistication, and just a dash of wickedness.

That went down very well, because this is just how most of us like to imagine ourselves.

"A dash of wickedness" here means the daring which prompts us to experiment with experiences we suspect are likely to burn our fingers. In our younger days we all have a built-in margin for this kind of experimentation: to eat this, smoke that, sniff this, experience that. Gradually, however, we need to learn that indulging such desires only leaves us hungrier than before.

In those days I had a young friend in Berkeley with an inordinate fondness for pastry. Delicacies of any kind had a hold on him, but Danish was his undoing. Unfortunately, on his way to work every morning he passed an excellent bakery – and every time he got on the bus, he confessed, he found himself polishing off a morning snack.

This kind of thing has never been a problem with me, so I began with what seemed obvious. "Are you hungry in the morning?" I asked. "Be sure you have a good, hearty breakfast before you set out."

"I tried that," he said. "I'm not hungry at all."

I must have looked puzzled. "It's not something I decide to do," he explained. "It just happens. I'm walking along the sidewalk with absolutely no intention of putting anything in my mouth, and as I pass by, not even glancing at the cherry strudel in the window, this invisible hand reaches out and drags me in. The next thing I know I'm back on the sidewalk with a white bag in my hand."

In my simplicity I suggested: "Why don't you just leave your wallet home?"

He looked aghast. "You mean you want me to steal?"

Most of us feel the same way about strong desires: we think we have no choice but to yield to them. But believe me, there is no joy in yielding to a compulsive desire. All yielding can do is give us a little respite from desire's demands – and make them stronger the next time. Joy comes not from yielding, but from gaining the freedom to choose.

When you have been meditating seriously for some time, for example, if you have a craving for alcohol or drugs, you can find a fierce thrill in just fighting it out. There is combativeness in our makeup not so we can fight others, but so we can take on these urges and see how much satisfaction we get in beating them.

Compulsive desires are part of the human condition, but today we have an additional problem: for almost all of us, our desires are exceptionally well trained. We send them to clinics where big-name trainers from the University of Madison Avenue coach them in what to crave. We buy them velour warm-up outfits with racy stripes, and shoes with aerodynamic design features that cost a hundred dollars. Just a hint of Pavlov's bell and they take off – and like runners in peak condition, they easily outstrip our will.

Recently I went to get some shoes that would be comfortable for walking. One pair fit well enough, so I asked the man the price. He replied, "Ninety-nine ninety-five."

"Dollars?"

He looked irritated.

"In India," I explained, "I could get comfortable shoes for just a fraction of that."

"Mister," he retorted, "there are shoes and *shoes*. With most shoes, after you put them on, you still have to move your feet. Put these on and they do the running for you."

That is the kind of shoes our desires sport these days. They take off running and we watch. We don't have to do a thing. The job of the will is to keep pace with desires and outrun them when necessary, but for most of us our will has been sleeping like Rip van Winkle. We drag him out in his pajamas and say, "Come on, Will, I need you to beat these desires!" But sometimes we can't even find the track.

When people want to give something up but say they just don't have the willpower, this is their situation: they do have a will; it just has to be trained. Meditation, as it turns out, is a perfect clinic. It has no self-interest; it operates solely on our own donations of enthusiasm.

I am not going to hide from you the fact that this training is going to be painful. Don't they say "No pain, no gain"? At the outset, every muscle in Will's flabby body is going to ache. But if you are resolute, he will begin to shed those excess pounds and approach the lean, sleek profile of a panther.

Training the will is such a serious topic that I might as well lighten it for a moment. Shaw once remarked that his method was to take pains to find the right thing to say and then to say it with the greatest levity. So in that vein, here is a cartoon I saw recently, probably in the *New Yorker*. A tortoise and a hare are dining in a Chinese restaurant, and both have just opened their fortune cookies. The tortoise reads aloud: "Slow and steady wins the race." He looks at the hare, and the hare says grumpily, "I refuse to disclose." You can guess.

In other words, don't start out by enrolling Will in the Boston Marathon. Train him steadily, every day. Eventually you will discover one of the most exhilarating secrets of life: there is no limit to the extent to which the human will can be trained.

In fact, the will has so much potential that eventually you can safely say, "It's true, I've given those desires a big head start. But I'm not worried. We're going to catch up." All desires know is to run flat out, so they don't even notice when Will begins to jog around the track. But gradually he gains speed, like a panther kept for a long time on a leash. He shoots around one final time, and when the tape comes into view no desires are in sight.

I hope I have made it clear that I am not anti-desires. It is just that I am so solidly pro-will. When your will is running smoothly in front, no desire can ever lead you around by the nose.

★

Training the will begins with making wise choices about where desires lead us – and practically speaking, that begins with food. Through choices about food, we begin to make choices about the mind.

This body of ours is made of food; that is the first reason why we have to be so careful about what we put into it. I do not go in for fads or fancies. I follow the advice of good nutritionists, who tell us in detail what is best for us to eat. Similarly, I like to think of myself as a sort of nutritionist for the mind. Selfishness, resentment, anger, lust – all these are junk food for the mind, and just as our body suffers setbacks on a steady diet of junk, the mind loses its balance and resiliency on a steady diet of junk thoughts.

When you go to a grocery store, don't you have a choice in what to place in your cart? We haven't yet reached a state in which the manager follows us around saying, "You have to buy two boxes of Crunchy Nuggets today." And if we do buy Crunchy Nuggets because they were right there by the cash register, no law says we have to put them in our mouth. With the body, then, making choices is relatively easy. But with the mind it is different. To paraphrase Augustine's poignant question: "When I tell my hand what to put in my mouth, it obeys. Why can't I tell my mind what to think?"

Now, the mind too is a kind of store. Consciousness, in fact, is the biggest chain store in the cosmos: an outlet in every individual mind. The Buddha calls this common or collective consciousness *alaya-vijnana*, "the store where thoughts are kept." By comparison, Safeway is just a mom-and-pop operation. The problem is that we don't mind our store. A double-trailer truck full of jealousy chips comes and we say, "Drop off as many cartons as you like. Can't stock too many of those!" Efficient grocery store managers simply would not work that way. They would say, "I didn't order that stuff, so get it out of here!"

Twenty-five years ago, when the ways of this country were still dawning on me, we used to pull into a gas station and see a little sign on top of the tank: "Free Tumbler with Fill-up." I used to ask my wife, "What is the tumbler for, to drink the gas?" I didn't see any connection.

That is the way junk thoughts appeal too. "Hey," jealousy says, "buy a few cartons of these, send in the tops, and we'll give your ego a rebate: fifty cents' worth of self-will." And we buy it. But fifty cents doesn't last long. Soon we find our mind full of junk anxieties, and the relationship we were agitated about is going downhill rapidly. Who was minding the store? When jealous thoughts appear at the loading dock of the mind, meditation enables you to say, "I never asked for you guys. Drop yourselves off at the nearest dump."

Scientists tell us that the body is constantly changing. New amino acids, minerals, and so on from the food we eat are always replacing what the body loses through wear and tear. Perhaps a sixth of the body gets turned over like this each year. At that rate, we get a completely new body every six years! By changing our eating habits, we could get just the body we want.

This may not be quite accurate where the body is concerned, but with the mind it is literally true. The mind *can* be replaced completely, just as you can replace the engine of your car. It takes much longer than six years to replace the store of consciousness with healthful, loving, healing thoughts, but it can be done. The key is knowing how to change your desires at will.

Desires that are good for our health, for our happiness, for our relationships, don't usually come attractively packaged. That is why we push them to the back of the shelf and put our energy into desires that promise fun. Here we need to develop some hardheaded business discrimination. We have to learn to evaluate everything – eating habits, work, entertainment, exercise – not for the immediate pleasure it promises, but for its long-term benefit or loss.

In other words, every desire has consequences that will affect our lives. One of the reasons I like to refer to Augustine is that as a young man, he was full of very human desires that we can readily understand. He was passionate about poetry, passionate about truth, passionate in his love affairs, and passionate to find God. These are desires with serious consequences, and until he was thirty or so, Augustine burnt his fingers badly. That is why his voice carries conviction when he tells us later that none of his experimentation with life's desires "brought fulfillment or peace of mind."

Everyone discovers this, the mystics say. Everyone suffers the consequences of desires that do not fulfill. But not everyone learns. That is the purpose of pain.

I have friends who would never have taken to meditation but for the load of suffering they bore for earlier escapades. Sometimes the burden is physical infirmity; more often it is emotional anguish. Worst of all is a sense of total alienation.

Most of these people found their burdens immensely eased by taking to meditation. Eventually they gained enough self-knowledge to say what every spiritual figure tries to pass on to us: "Blessed be the day I suffered so much, because it forced me to search for God."

★

Not all powerful desires, of course, are harmful in where they lead. One deep desire which plays a vital role in spiritual evolution is what Sir Peter Medawar, the distinguished British biologist, called the "rage to know." This is not an insatiable curiosity about facts and circumstances, but a driving need to understand the secrets of life. It can produce great scientists, but it also produces great philosophers and mystics; for it is this same desire that makes us yearn to know for certain what life is and whether it has a purpose, and what, if anything, awaits us after death.

Pursuing this deep desire is a little like breaking codes. When I was a Boy Scout, I once astonished my grandmother by talking to a cousin just by waving two flags. "My scoutmaster taught me a secret code," I explained. I don't think she knew what I was talking about; she wasn't terribly interested in codes. But she knew how to read all the codes of life, which the vast majority of us never suspect.

I remember vividly the morning our scoutmaster took a small patrol of us tramping into the tropical forest a few miles from our village. A man from a forest tribe came with us as our guide, and although he evidently felt ill at ease in our village, he was as much at home in the forest as I felt in my own room. We would be crashing along behind him and suddenly he would stop and say, "Shhh, listen! There's a tiger." We couldn't make out a thing. But to him every sound was a message, in a language we couldn't even hear.

For most of us, a moment comes at least once – perhaps a loved one dies, or life deals a blow that dashes our hopes to pieces – when we pause to reflect, and questions float up into our minds: "What has happened to my friend? I was with him only last week; where is he now?" "My lover is gone; is this the end of our love?" And perhaps the lines from Omar Khayyám spring to mind:

There was the door to which I found no key:
There was the veil through which I could not see:
Some little talk awhile of me and thee
There was – and then no more of thee and me.

When questions like these arise, we often plunge into distractions in order to forget again, pretending that life on earth is not a profound riddle whose solution matters. But some people pursue the questions. They go on to ask themselves: *Why am I here? Why is there so much sorrow and violence in the world? Why do children die?* And they cannot rest until their questions get answered. These are people who, more than anything else in life, want to understand.

For this kind of deep understanding, we have to break the code of desires; for it is only when desire is understood and mastered that life's meaning can be seen. This is the purpose of meditation, which plumbs the depths of consciousness where our deep desires arise. In its climax we grasp at last the secret that Augustine hinted at in such deceptively simple words: "How can I find rest anywhere else, Lord, when I am made to rest in thee?"

All desire, the ancient codebooks of the scriptures suggest, arises ultimately from the sense of being a finite individual, separated and estranged from the whole. There is a kind of primal loneliness about this state, a hunger for reunion, that is expressed in the myth of Eden I referred to in the first pages of this book. In the mysticism of Christianity, Judaism, and Islam, the apple of the Fall is the temptation to think of ourselves as separate creatures, whose first concern is personal satisfaction. From the loneliness that gripped Adam and Eve in the wake of this first isolation in themselves – and which grips the rest of us who follow them – arose the haunting conclusion that prompts all human desires: "I am alone, separate from the universe, and I feel hungry and incomplete. Therefore, what can complete me, what can fill my hunger, must be waiting for me somewhere outside."

In evolutionary terms, this root loneliness is a force four and a half billion years old – as old as life itself. Ultimately, it is behind all our attempts to fulfill ourselves in the world outside us. Yet it is an extremely positive power, for it also drives the struggle for reintegration which motivates spiritual and cultural growth.

How is it that this deep desire for reintegration, essentially the same in all of us, expresses itself so differently in different individuals? The answer is that this root desire arrives at the threshold of our everyday awareness only after being filtered through various layers of personality. These are the strata of personal and biological conditioning – drives, habits, aversions, and so on – that give each of us our own particular personality profile.

Like strata of the earth's surface, the mystics would say, this profile is the record not just of one lifetime, but of thousands of years of biological conditioning over the course of evolution. Such layers acknowledge the heritage of our jungle ancestry; but it is equally accurate, in spiritual terms, to say that they trace the path we have wandered for eons from the Garden of original fulfillment.

In Sanskrit, these layers of conditioning are called *koshas:* sheaths or jackets that cover our real Self. They are five. Innermost is what might be called the ego-sheath, for it imposes the sense of separateness, the sense of "I." But in Sanskrit it is also called the "sheath of joy," because at this level, consciousness is so rarefied that only a little sense of a limited personality separates us from our real Self.

Outside this level of awareness lies what is sometimes called the "higher mind," the seat of clear understanding, judgment, and will. This layer, in turn, is covered by the "lower mind," the turbulent region of our emotional life. Enveloping this is the layer of sensory awareness. And outermost of all is the only component of personality that we can see: the physical body. All these levels have habits and conditioning of their own, which affects the way life's basic desires find individual expression.

When I was a boy, I was delighted the first time I saw a prism take clear sunlight and spread it in a rainbow of colors across our school wall. These sheaths of consciousness, too, act as planes in a prism, scattering a unitary spiritual yearning into a million different emotional and physical desires.

In each of us, then, what starts out as a simple longing for unity becomes particularized. We see it through the fantasies and emotions of the mind, then try to satisfy those emotional needs with sensory satisfactions in this particular physical frame which we believe is what we are. We try to fill ourselves by eating, to forget ourselves in drinking, to find our home in the universe by traveling, to complete ourselves through physical union with another human being who is searching for the same thing. Through these filters, what begins as a simple appreciation of the beauty in another person may end as a compulsion to possess – and the more we clutch, the less we find; for no one can rob beauty and have it for his own.

I confess that in my university days, even though I had read about these forces, I too did not suspect that they might be as real as the force of gravity. Still less would I have understood that they are resources of infinite power from which any human being can learn to draw. Today I know these things from personal experience. It is my spiritual teacher, my grandmother, who showed me what a vast world of love and creativity the human being can command when the immense power of our original goodness is tapped and directed toward a lofty spiritual goal.

★

To undo the conditioning imposed by these planes of personality, we begin by redirecting where our desires go. More easily said than done! Even a strong will is not always enough to accomplish this kind of mental engineering. What meditation allows us to do, one step at a time, is to climb down into consciousness as we would into a deep swimming pool, so that over years of practice we manage to enter the levels where particular desires arise. Only from these depths can we resist a misdirected desire and direct its power wisely.

Sensory attractions may seem compelling, but compared with deeper desires they really have little power. Even when they seem overwhelming, as with my friend's attraction to Danish pastry, their power over us really comes from a deeper stratum of personality – often, for example, from our emotional needs. It is in the filter of emotional attachments that most of our personal difficulties arise. And most strong emotional attachments get their strength largely from our thinking about ourselves.

Thoughts, that is, gain power from the attention we give them. Every time we start turning over in our minds sixteen ways to fulfill a cherished desire, that desire puts on weight; that is, it gets that much more power to force us to do what it demands. If we think about it all the time, it becomes huge like a Japanese sumo wrestler. That is a compulsion.

Most of the energy we spend on daydreaming, rehashing the past, planning a future tailor-made for ourselves, is at best a waste of energy. At worst it locks us further into habits we want to change.

Letting the mind idle with its desires running is like letting your car sit out all night with the engine running: when you want to get going in the morning, you are out of gas. Worse, when the mind is left unattended like this, any passing desire can just climb in and take off. Then you find yourself walking out of the bar or the pizza parlor wondering, "Why did I go and do that?"

One of the reasons why repeating the Holy Name can be so effective is simply that it saves so much wasted mental energy. When the mind wants to run on about something that is neither useful nor beneficial, we can learn to start up the Holy Name and turn the key of this enormous mental engine to Off.

Once you taste this blissful stillness, you know you are not your thoughts. That is a tremendous achievement, for it brings access to the limitless resources of the unconscious.

The University of California at Berkeley, as you may know, has one of the finest research libraries in the world, but undergraduate students can benefit from it only partially. They are not allowed into the library stacks, so they have to stand in line to petition the clerks to get a book for them, and then pray the book is in. But graduate students are not subjected to these indignities. All they have to do is flash their card and the clerk at the gate will wave them through. Then they can wander through the books at will, nine tiers of shelves, marveling at what they find and picking out whatever they need.

That is how it is when you know you are not your thoughts: you get a security clearance into the deepest resources of consciousness. You don't have to petition for more patience and then wait and pray it will come. You can go straight in, deep in meditation, and when you reach the tollgate of the unconscious, you just establish your identity and your mind will wave you through.

We may not know it, we may not believe it, but in our hearts every one of us longs to get at the immense wealth of the world within. Even the lady who goes to play blackjack every weekend is looking to break the bank inside, the infinite treasury of love which is our legacy as human beings. In other words, all of us want to love and be loved. When we have removed all the jealousy and greed and resentment in our hearts, what remains is pure love.

As we descend into the depths of the mind in meditation, we gradually strip away layer on layer of selfish conditioning. Why should anybody love us when the only thing we are concerned about is ourselves? Care for others, share with others, even if it means ignoring your own comforts and pursuits and urges; then people will naturally love and cherish you. When you make yourself zero, Gandhi would say, the Lord adds an infinity of digits beyond.

"Be ye therefore perfect," Jesus challenges us, "even as your Father which is in heaven is perfect." It means: Let's see you really exercise your courage, stretch your patience, deepen your love beyond limit. Life will supply opportunities in plenty. If you want spiritual growth, there is no need to retire to a wilderness hermitage or even to a tree house in your backyard. We can reach for perfection right in the middle of life, while holding down a responsible job.

But who has the energy for this kind of effort? Even if we do want to reach beyond ourselves, which of us has the vitality, endurance, and dedication? The mystics are so full of vitality that we may think we have to be born like them in order to follow in their footsteps. Fortunately, it isn't so. Every one of us has access to deep reserves of vital energy of which we are largely unaware.

Gandhi, in his seventies, used to work hard for fifteen hours a day seven days a week. Often he and his staff would not get to bed until midnight, but he would rouse everyone at three in the morning to get going again; there was work to do. That is *your* capacity too, he used to tell us. We have learned to use only a small fraction of what we have.

Where did Gandhi get those tremendous reserves of energy? Not from being frugal about using it, obviously, since he poured his heart into energetic effort right and left for decades. Rather, he got his vitality from spending it.

I know this sounds like a plain contradiction, but that is

precisely how vitality works. Just as athletes train their bodies, we can train the mind until it becomes marvelously fuel-efficient. Few effects of meditation are more dramatic.

I have always been a hard worker, like my mother and especially my grandmother. Yet I am the first person to be amazed to see that today, at an age when most men have retired, I have immeasurably more vitality than I did in my twenties. I work longer and much more effectively, but without fatigue or burnout, and I need only a few hours of sleep a night. After decades of training in meditation, there is no agitation in my mind; so very little energy leaks out.

The secret is simple: I seldom think about myself. This is what drains vitality, because it is dwelling on ourselves that churns the mind with excitement, craving, anxiety, competition, and disappointment. If you want a life full of vitality, the mystics say, don't waste your energy in thinking about yourself. Think about others. You will find it not only conserves personal energy, it actually brings you to life.

The thrust of our contemporary civilization is just the opposite. "Don't ever forget your personal needs," popular magazines warn, "or you'll become a zombie." Saint Francis would say this is picking up the stick by the wrong end. If we want our personality to shine, to be aflame with beauty, we must learn to love. "O divine Master, grant that I may not so much seek to be consoled as to console, to be understood as to understand, to be loved as to love." This is the formula for a personality that draws all hearts, and its secret lies in forgetting ourselves in working for the welfare of all.

Saint Francis, Gandhi, Saint Teresa – far from being zombies, great lovers of God like these are among the most original figures in history. They burst on the world with the vitality of a dozen ordinary souls. Every one of us, they testify, has this kind of vitality in abundance; we simply do not know how to get at it. That is the purpose of meditation.

Ultimately, all the energy that drives the functions of life comes from a single source, a vast kind of reserve of undifferentiated power. We can think of this energy as an immense trust fund of "evolutionary energy," kept in a cosmic bank. At birth a checking account is opened in our name, credited with a certain measure of vital energy – not a large amount, but enough to see us through the ordinary energy expenses of our life. To this minimum, the bank in its mercy credits a little extra to cover the mistakes most of us make in learning to invest.

From birth to death, this modest checking account is all the vitality we have to draw on. We never suspect there is any more. Yet this is only the interest on a vast cosmic trust, which the bank is just waiting for us to come of age and claim. As with a financial legacy, we need to establish our credentials before we can make withdrawals. And the main credential is that we be living for all. For this vast account is held in trust for all of life. It becomes available to us only when we have a deep need to give to others and have reached the limits of what we can draw on in ourselves.

Gandhi drew on this cosmic account every day, and it allowed him to accomplish almost superhuman things. Another way of putting it is to say that Gandhi had learned to tap the power that lies in the very depths of the unconscious. Or, following Saint Teresa of Avila, we might speak of a perpetual wellspring of grace, from which the soul can always go to be filled from within. "He leadeth me beside the still waters," says David. "He restoreth my soul." This endless pool of vitality is there for every one of us to tap, if we can only find and uncover it.

This is what is meant by making ourselves "pure in heart." When we practice meditation, repeat the mantram, and put the welfare of others before our personal interests, we are digging for this spring of living waters, removing all the strata of self-will and selfishness that cover it. In the end, the mystics of all religions say, it is not we who actually open up this spring. That is up to the Lord, who is within. But we have to make all the effort. Our job is to purify the mind, to get every obstruction out of the way.

★

For the vast majority of human beings, the strongest urge is sex. Very few today understand that when the mystics harp on the need to master sexual desire, it is not because sex is "wrong" but because this deepest of urges is an immense source of power. Such is the pull of sexual desire that it lays down a direct track into the unconscious. This is the secret of its strength: it draws straight from the treasury of power in the unconscious, the longing for fulfillment that reaches back into Eden in the depths of the heart.

The difficulty with handling this secret channel of power is that until sexual desire is mastered, it moves down a one-way street. We have no say in where it takes us; it just grabs us, throws us in the trunk, and takes off with the accelerator pedal on the floor. Before we know it, we are dumped back where we started, often with some souvenirs of the Land of Physical Desire – jealousy and insecurity – slipped into our luggage.

In meditation we slowly gain the capacity to buck the flow of this fierce traffic. Meditation is a kind of mental engineering project, laying down a lane by which we can, when we choose, travel back against the flow of conditioning into the realms of the unconscious, where our deepest resources lie. This does not mean sex is stifled; it simply means we have a choice. We can use it for a few moments of personal pleasure, or we can draw on its power to make a lasting contribution to the rest of life.

Given the conditioning of our times, I think it is only natural to think of sex in terms of private satisfaction, particularly in youth. In his compassion the Lord gives us leeway for experimentation, so that we can learn for ourselves how little the senses can really gratify. But as we grow older, we are expected to learn from our experiences and set our aspirations on a higher goal. When this happens, we begin to look everywhere for more gas, more drive, more love with which to solve the problems that living poses. And no source is greater than sexual desire.

In the Indian scriptures, sex is evolutionary energy. Its physical expression is only the tip of the immense iceberg in consciousness which is pure desire. Locked within it is the creative drive behind evolution, so intensely compressed that when this drive is released and harnessed, it can shoot us straight to heaven. This power is our rocket to the stars. But its evolutionary purpose is wasted on the pursuit of pleasure. If we really want to grow spiritually, we have to learn to master this immense source of power; otherwise toward the end of our lives we may find ourselves without enough gas to reach our goal. As you can see, this is not a moral issue; it is essentially a matter of spiritual engineering.

Mahatma Gandhi had a grand insight which I didn't even begin to understand until I went deep in meditation. When sexual desire comes under complete control, he said, it turns into longing for God. That one observation explains why those who offer their whole life, all their desires, to the Lord are not suppressing their faculties or stunting their humanity. On the contrary, by drawing on this endless tank of energy that is sexual desire they bring all their faculties into glorious play.

In Hindu mythology the god of physical passion,

called Kama, has five flower-tipped arrows in his quiver. They look pretty, but as all of us know, they go in deep. These arrows correspond to the five senses, but they can also be described as five aftereffects of overindulgence in sex: jealousy, insecurity, loss of freedom, enervation, and loneliness. Similarly, what we get when we transform this energy are five incomparable boons: vitality, security, creative freedom, emotional endurance, and compassion for all.

In every religion, the mystics assure us that through many years of hard work – of intense meditation and continuous striving – all desires can be brought together, to flow like the Amazon River from an endless spring of love within. When you can give your devotion completely to the Lord in the depths of your heart, you will have an eternal source of inspiration, creativity, and joy, "a well of water springing up into everlasting life."

★

I have a number of teenage friends, and in some ways I think teenagers see through the allure of sex better than those who are older and more experienced. Young people can be sensitive and sharp-eyed. They look around and see where the pursuit of pleasure has taken the previous generation, and I believe they are ready to understand that to love deeply, the sexual faculty has to come gradually under control. To love, you have to banish jealousy; you have to rise above possessiveness. In other words, you need to see the other person as more than just a physical creature.

Love takes a lot of effort. A self-centered Romeo cannot love. All he can promise is: "I love you, Juliet . . . as long as I am the center of your universe and you keep orbiting around me."

Yet love is what everyone wants, and young people in

particular need to be shown that it is worth working for. This is the responsibility of those of us who have lived longer, who have burnt our fingers enough to know what physical passion can and cannot give. No matter what we preach at young people, it is our example that they watch, in our lives and in the mirror of the media. If we want a world with a goal higher than pleasure, we have to strive for it in our own lives. It is my fervent hope that thousands of young people in this country who have not yet become entangled in sex as a compulsion can learn to transform this force and become powers for love.

I want to repeat some lines from Mechthild of Magdeburg, a lay sister in a Cistercian abbey in Thuringia, central Germany, and a contemporary of Eckhart's, who gives us the reason for our soul's need for love:

> I was created in love; therefore nothing can console or liberate me save love alone. The soul is formed of love and must ever strive to return to love. Therefore it can never find rest nor happiness in other things. It must lose itself in love.

God is home, Augustine says brilliantly; all of us are abroad. We are perpetual tourists in this world, gazing wonderingly at all the strange sights. Only when we get tired of sightseeing do we begin to look for a way to get home.

Nothing more transfigures the human spirit than when all personal desires fuse in the desire to return to our native state of unitive consciousness. Far from being self-indulgent, this is the highest ambition imaginable. It enables us to hope and work and live for making our world a little better for others to live in, particularly the children who will follow us. And it leads, in the end, to the highest summit of awareness that a human being can reach for, the Mount Everest of the spirit.

Not long ago a friend of mine was going to India and

asked if he could take a message for me. I said, "Give my love to the Himalayas." How can one convey the splendor of mountain ranges that spread over fifteen hundred miles across the roof of the world, with peak after peak above twenty thousand feet? The first time I saw them, it was not only their height that stunned me but their unutterable purity – so pure that it seemed to enter my heart. *Himalaya* literally means "the home of snow." It is the purity of this perpetual snow that makes the Himalayas the perfect symbol of the eternal home in our hearts which we call God.

George Mallory, who made the first recorded ascent of Mount Everest in 1924, was asked by journalists why he felt he had to risk his life on an impossible challenge. Mallory gave an epic reply: "Because it is there." Millions of people hear reports of the Himalayas but nothing stirs inside them. Most of us are so engrossed with playing pigeon on the plains, picking up whatever crumbs of satisfaction we can find, that we never think of the words of the Psalms: "I will lift up mine eyes unto the hills, from whence cometh my help" – the towering mountains of the spirit, wrapped in perpetual purity. Mallory was one of those rare individuals who lifted up his eyes and felt a deep inner stirring which would not let him live in peace. He died making his ascent, but his courage lit a path for others to follow to the top.

To me, this is the real glory of human nature. "Let there be dangers; bring them on! I don't ask for a guided tour with a guarantee of success; all I ask is the strength and courage to go on trying. I want more than anything else to live to the full height of my being." Self-realization can be attained only by facing difficulties which appear to be almost impossible. That's why I often poke fun at the words "fun" and "pleasure." Once you raise your eyes, what satisfaction can you get from pecking about on the plains? It is challenge that makes a human being glow, effort that hardens our muscles, danger that fuses our dedication and desire.

Many more attempts to climb Everest followed Mallory's, until in 1953, Sir Edmund Hillary and Tenzing Norgay reached the summit for the first time in history. I still remember the enthusiasm with which my students in India responded to the news. One day, I thought to myself, I hope to have the privilege of teaching young people the exploits of great mountaineers of the spirit: climbers like Mechthild, Eckhart, Gandhi, Saint Teresa, Saint Francis. I think it was a young woman from Berkeley who, after she reached the crest of Everest herself, coined a slogan I still see on T-shirts: A Woman's Place Is at the Top. I say, "Right on! And a man's place is right there beside her." Nobody should ever be content to crawl on the ground looking for the crumbs of pleasure that life offers. The place of every one of us is at the summit of living.

In meditation we learn to reach into consciousness, get hold of our biggest desires, and fuse them into an irresistible force that can lift us like an eagle, as Saint Teresa says, and carry us to the peak of spiritual awareness. It is not a luxury for our civilization to hold out this goal; it has become a necessity. When human beings reach a state where physical wants are more than satisfied, if they do not have a lofty, snow-clad peak to gaze on, to plan for, and to climb, they cannot help indulging in destructive behavior. Human daring is meant for this purpose, and if we do not engage it, all that power will turn against us. The social problems which challenge our future – drugs, violence, AIDS, alienation, war, the despoliation of the environment – all, in the end, are fed by desires turned desperate because they can be fulfilled only on higher ground.

Something in the human spirit demands to challenge impossible odds. One of the sages in the Upanishads tells us what the climb to the summit of consciousness is like. "Don't expect a path of convenient rocks," he says.

"You'll have to climb up the edge of a razor." This is the path of glory that all of us are born for, our path to a beauty and a joy which cannot be imagined.

Mahatma Gandhi stirred me like this; that is why I talk about him so much. Here was a man barely five and a half feet tall, but when I set eyes on him he seemed to tower above the rest of us like the Himalayas. Something stirred deep within me, as if to say: *That is my destiny too: to stand where I can see all people as my people, all countries as my own. That is my home.*

Two or three years ago, along with thousands of others in the San Francisco area, I awoke one morning to read in the paper that in the course of its long swim home, a humpback whale had somehow got in through the Golden Gate and was trapped in the shallows of the Sacramento River Delta. These majestic, sensitive creatures, who come to us from fathomless depths like visiting rulers from a kingdom we can never see, stir the unconscious. Humphrey the humpback caught the city's heart, for without deep waters no whale can thrive.

For almost a week, while the papers had a field day, Humphrey could not be coaxed from his new bathtub back to the sea. Finally somebody got the bright idea of enticing him with the recorded underwater songs of whale Loreleis. They must have picked the right tunes for awakening nostalgia, because Humphrey leaped and turned and began to make his way to freedom, distracted only momentarily by the inexplicable lure of the Richmond Bridge. As he churned triumphantly out the mouth of the bay, traffic backed up in both directions while whale-lovers stopped in the middle of the Golden Gate Bridge and stood at the railing to cheer.

We are like that, the mystics would tell us: great creatures made to roam in the deep waters of the spirit, caught in the shallows of a narrow vision of who we are. Yet in the voices of the mystics and scriptures, the echoes from poetry and myth, we hear "deep calling unto deep." Wordsworth records it in his suggestively titled "Intimations of Immortality":

> Hence in a season of calm weather
> Though inland far we be,
> Our Souls have sight of that immortal sea
> Which brought us hither,
> Can in a moment travel thither,
> And see the Children sport upon the shore,
> And hear the mighty waters rolling evermore.

Midnight or early morning, while the world sleeps, when awareness of the outside world falls away in profound meditation, these words may come to life. Then you will see the "immortal sea which brought us hither," will hear it calling; and you will see too the way back to your real home.

When we regain our native state of unity, we ask nothing more of life. It is not that the spirit of searching is dead: spiritual fulfillment is not the end of growth, only a new beginning. But we no longer ask who we are and why we are here; we know. And in place of the world that once baffled and frustrated us, we dwell in a compassionate universe whose forces are friendly once they are understood.

"Having this," the Bhagavad Gita says, "what more is there to ask for?" All we need is opportunities to give, to serve, to love – which is, without exaggeration, to live in Eden here on earth.

Reading the Mystics

ONE OF MY HOPES in writing this book was that the quotations I chose might stir some readers to explore for themselves the poetry, power, and contemporary relevance of the world's great mystics.

To me, reading the mystics is not merely a pleasure; it plays a vital role in spiritual growth. Until we turn inward in meditation, most of us cannot guess how thoroughly the mass media have saturated our minds with a low, purely physical image of human nature. To undo this conditioning, these images must be erased from consciousness and replaced by the loftiest ideals to which we can aspire. This is the job of meditation and the Holy Name. But their work becomes infinitely easier if we start saying no to some of the tawdry stuff that goes into the mind through our eyes and ears, and replace it with the inspiring words and personal example of men and women whose love of God can set fire to our lives.

That is why, whenever I teach meditation, I always make spiritual reading one of my eight essential points. After your evening meditation, instead of stirring your mind up again with the violence and vulgarity on TV, go to bed with a book of pure spiritual inspiration – not philosophy or psychology, however helpful these may be at other times, but the direct words or life of someone who has realized God.

★

I confess that I rarely recommend books *on* mysticism, preferring to go straight to the sources. Nevertheless, there are at least three books which let the mystics speak for themselves in a readable and reliable setting: *The Perennial Philosophy*, by Aldous Huxley (Harper, 1945), *Mysticism*, by Evelyn Underhill (Dutton, 1961, first published 1911), and *Mysticism: A Study and an Anthology,* by F. C. Happold (Penguin, 1970).

Of the individual mystics I quote in this book, almost all can be found in the Paulist Press "Classics of Western Spirituality" series, now the best source for Christian (and some Jewish and Islamic) mystics otherwise out of print: Ruysbroeck, Juliana of Norwich, Origen, and many others, including the anonymous works *Cloud of Unknowing* and *Theologia Germanica*, misleadingly listed in this series under the authorship of Martin Luther. Some, true classics, are available in many other editions as well: Augustine's *Confessions*, Brother Lawrence's *Practice of the Presence of God*, Thomas a Kempis's *Imitation of Christ*, and the works of the great Spanish mystics Teresa of Avila and John of the Cross. The mysticism of the early church is well represented in *The Desert Fathers*, translated with an excellent introduction by Helen Waddell (University of Michigan Press, Ann Arbor Paperbacks, 1957).

Meister Eckhart in particular has benefited from new translations. My quotations are based on that of Raymond Blakney (*Meister Eckhart: A Modern Translation*, Harper, 1941), which I have used for decades. But devoted scholarship has since produced a solid critical edition of Eckhart's works, and readers today can take advantage of two new English translations: *Meister Eckhart*, translated with an introduction by Edmund Colledge and Bernard McGinn (Paulist Press, Classics of Western Spirituality series, 1981), and the three-volume edition by Maurice O'Connell Walshe (*Meister Eckhart: Sermons & Treatises*, Shaftesbury, England, Element Books, 1987).

Quotations from the Indian scriptures are from my own translations, *Bhagavad Gita* (Petaluma, Calif., Nilgiri Press, 1985) and *Upanishads* (1987), both of which have introductions and notes presenting the key ideas of Indian mysticism to the Western reader. The quotations from Mahatma Gandhi are from my *Gandhi the Man* (Nilgiri Press, 1977), which is neither biography nor anthology but seeks to understand how Gandhi transformed his personality. Many other selections from Gandhi are in print. Of the many biographies, Louis Fischer's *Gandhi: His Life and Message for the World* (Mentor, 1945) still gives one of the most sensitive introductions to Gandhi's life.

The Prayer of Jesus, probably used in the times of the Desert Fathers, is enjoying new popularity today, partly because of the underground classic *The Way of a Pilgrim* (translated by R. M. French, many editions). A good historical account is *The Jesus Prayer*, by "A Monk of the Eastern Church" (Crestwood, N.Y., St. Vladimir's Seminary Press, 1987). But for practical use of the Prayer, or for repetition of the Holy Name in any other form, I recommend my own *Mantram Handbook* (Nilgiri Press, 1977), which is written not for monks and nuns but for ordinary lay people in the modern world. It is accessible to anyone and full of examples from personal experience.

Index

Index

Index

Index

Middle Ages, 12

military, 170, 171, 201

mind: death &, 174; dynamics of, 60, 108, 123, 155, 163, 217; depths of, 44, 116, 152, 157, 173, 195, 198, 210, 218; distorts, 33–39, 116, 178, 180, 216; forces of, 133–135, 157, 182, 194; habits of, 55, 113, 127, 135, 153, 154, 178, 199; health &, 100–101, 112, 164; higher"& "lower", 115; mantram &, *see* Mantram, Holy Name; meditation &, *see* Meditation; native state of consciousness &, 22, 75; negative thoughts in, 46, 67, 75, 100, 101, 103, 107, 112, 123, 132–135, 178, 210–211; one-pointed, 26, 157; peace in, 62, 63, 109, 111, 118, 178, 196; positive states of, 100, 133, 135, 155, 196, 199; pure, 33, 38, 39, 44, 164, 222; simplicity &, 87; speed of, 67-68, 69, 105, 108, 110; still, 39, 67, 106, 118; stress &, 100–104; time &, 66, 67; training the, 26, 27, 66, 68, 72, 99–111, 114, 125–128, 131, 137, 157, 179, 196, 197–200, 210, 220; vital energy &, 106, 154, 155, 159, 217, 220; wandering, 25, 86, 156

mistrust, 153, 162, 187–188. *See also* Trust

motivation, 73, 83, 188, 192, 197, 193, 215

movies, 160

multiplicity, 50, 96

mystics & mysticism, 12, 23, 42, 131, 142, 213: defined, 9; character of, 82, 115, 146, 147, 219; perspective of, on love 96, 126, 137, 139, 149, 150, on sorrow 99, 129, on human nature & capacities, 9, 17, 20, 22, 29, 56, 95, 115, 141, 158, 228, on peace 177, 178, on mind & consciousness 32–36, 38, 39, 55, 75, 105, 180, 194, on sex 222, 224, on physical & spiritual realities, 32, 134; reading in the, 75, 231–232. *See also* Christian mystics; Jewish mystics & mysticism; *etc.*

nature, 22, 40, 59; human, *see* Human being, nature of

New Age ideas, 11, 14

Newton, Sir Isaac, 133–134

nirvana, 64

noise, 103

nonviolence, 134, 165–170, 180, 182

Norgay, Tenzing, 227

Now, the eternal, 66

nuclear war & weapons, 15, 83, 102, 171, 183, 185, 186, 188, 203

obsession, 21, 80, 151, 163

obstacles, spiritual, 43, 61, 122, 128, 222

oceans, 89

Omar Khayyam, 213

opinions, 58, 70, 187

opportunities, spiritual, 91, 95, 219: for forgiveness, 138; for giving & helping, 120, 139, 146, 229; for love, 122, 124; for mantram, 46; for patience, 113, 114; for peace, 188, 200

opposition, 58, 71, 144, 179

Origen, 10

"original goodness," 9–13, 16, 17, 22, 29, 33, 54, 149, 216

overeating, 84, 195

pain, 98: at death, 174; Christ's, 161; conditioning &, 117; in spiritual growth, 122, 128, 144, 209; is unavoidable, 98, 123; mantram &, 73; purpose of, 118, 119, 128, 212; self-will &, 73–74, 75. *See also* Suffering

Palme, Olaf, 201

parents, 71, 87, 115, 189, 190

passage, meditation, 27, 28, 29, 43, 65, 67, 74, 100, 101, 114, 198

Passion (Christ's), 129, 130, 161

passions, 39, 44, 127, 157, 175, 179, 200

past, 11, 66–67, 74, 133, 153, 162, 163, 172, 173, 174, 217

Patanjali, 200

patience, 46, 66, 111–116, 139, 155, 181, 219; suffering &, 128, 138

Paul, St., 82, 144, 151

peace & peacemaking, 152, 170, 177–194, 196, 199, 200–202: anger &, 165, 178–179, 200, 201; of mind, *see* Mind, peace in; training the mind &, 165, 177–180, 193–194, 196

Pearce, Joseph Chilton, 183, 184, 187

Peattie, Lisa, 201

perception, 33–38, 104

personality, 11, 192: conflicts in, 25; core of, 8, 14, 136, 192, 193; death &, 173, 174; health &, 104, 110; levels of, 33, 215–216; meditation &, 25, 26; transformation of, 42, 62, 65, 82, 142, 200, 220

physics, 16, 17, 34, 36, 134

pilgrimage of the soul, 20

pleasure, 13, 32, 105–107, 110, 164, 192: Eckhart on, 99; John of the Cross on, 81; pain &, 120, 124, 128; sex &, 223–224; supreme goal &, 9, 14, 191, 212, 223–227

pollution, 78, 87, 88, 89, 92, 94, 98, stress of 102, 103; mental, 133, 135, 154

poor, the, 171, 172, 188

"poor in spirit," 56, 64, 81

Pope John Paul II, 85

possessions, 14, 22, 81, 98, 131, 192: John of the Cross on, 81

possessiveness, 216, 224

potential, human, *see* Human being, capacities of

prana, 154, 160

prayer: interior, 24; from Rig Veda, 96; Gandhi on, 44, 74; of Jesus, 45; of St. Francis, 28, 43, 65, 114; the Lord's, 46, 64

presence of God, 9, 44, 47; Shekinah as, 17

present moment, 66–67, 148

pressure, emotional, 111, 155, 159, 193

priorities, peace &, 171, 173, 174, 184, 191

production, industrial, 79–80, 85–89

profit, 13, 189, 191, 192

progress, 13, 100; toward peace, 170, 179, 186

Psalms, quoted, 46, 79, 175, 221

Index